Learning about Food and Beverage Service

John Cousins and

Robert Smith

Thames Valley University,
Ealing, London
and Slough, Berkshire

&

Birmingham College
of Food, Tourism and
Creative Studies

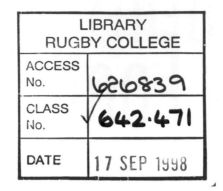
Orders: please contact Bookpoint Ltd, 39 Milton Park, Abingdon, Oxon OX14 4TD. Telephone: (44) 01235 400414, Fax: (44) 01235 400454. Lines are open from 9.00 – 6.00, Monday to Saturday, with a 24 hour message answering service. Email address: orders@bookpoint.co.uk

British Library Cataloguing in Publication Data
A catalogue record for this title is available from the British Library

ISBN 0 340 70530 2

First Published 1998
Impression number   10   9   8   7   6   5   4   3   2   1
Year   2004   2003   2002   2001   2000   1999   1998

Cover photos by Owen Franken

Typeset by Wearset, Boldon, Tyne and Wear.
Printed in Great Britain for Hodder & Stoughton Educational, a division of Hodder Headline Plc, 338 Euston Road, London NW1 3BH by Scotprint Ltd, Musselburgh, Scotland.

CONTENTS

ACKNOWLEDGEMENTS

The authors would like to thank all those who helped with the preparation of this text. In particular we would like to thank Andrew Durkan, author and consultant, formerly of Ealing College, London and Dennis Lillicrap, author and consultant, formerly of Thames Valley University. Additionally we would like to acknowledge the use of information from the Académie Culinaire de France (UK); the Academy of Food and Wine Service; the City and Guilds of London Institute; Hospitality and Leisure Manpower; Hospitality Skills; the Hospitality Training Foundation; the Restaurateurs' Association of Great Britain; the Savoy Education Trust and the Wine and Spirit Education Trust.

INTRODUCTION

Working in food and beverage service offers a wealth of opportunity for professional development and advancement. Eating away from home is generally increasing, and the nature and type of food and beverages on offer are also developing.

Because of the expansion of the industry and increasing pressures for improved professionalism in food and beverage service staff, there is an even greater need for more people to make their careers in this profession. Alongside this comes the need for improved confidence and performance through higher standards of knowledge and skills. For those committed to our industry, and to working in food and beverage service, a fulfilling, exciting and enjoyable career awaits.

This book has been designed to help in the development of an individual learning programme for those who wish to develop their knowledge, skill, experience and careers in food and beverage service. It is intended to be used as a learning guide together with two text books: *Food and Beverage Service* and *The Beverage Book* (although both these books can be used independently) and references are made to these two books throughout this text.

The individual learning programme can also be used by those who are wishing to be assessed at Levels 1, 2 and 3 of the National Vocational Qualifications (NVQ and including the Scottish SVQ) in food and beverage service and for a range of other qualifications, including the City and Guilds of London Institute 7066, Certificate, Diploma or Advanced Diploma in Food and Beverage Service (see Section 1).

This book is therefore suitable for

- students studying food and beverage service where the text is used to support individual learning or is being used as part of a course
- those working in food and beverage service to support their individual learning or where the text is being used as the basis for an employer training programme

Sections 1 to 3 of this book are introductory and provide advice about working in the industry, the qualifications, how to identify learning needs, undertake learning activities and to record achievement. There are also printed record forms which may be photocopied up to A4.

Sections 4 to 10 provide advice on learning about the various aspects of food and beverage service, and each Section includes suggested learning activities which are designed to help develop skills and knowledge.

The Sections follow a logical progression from underpinning knowledge through to service skills and on to their application into a variety of service situations. Supervisory aspects are then considered in Section 10. The supervisory aspects which are covered are those related most closely to the books *Food and Beverage Service* and *The Beverage Book*. Thus, for instance, personnel issues are not fully covered in this text, as there is a wide range of other support materials available for human resource management.

The suggested learning activities can be related to the assessment requirements of the NVQ standards and the records of achievement can be used as evidence of fulfilling assessment requirements. The learning activities and records of achievement can also be used as part of an employer or college-based course leading to a range of other qualifications.

This book can only be a guide. It is not intended to be prescriptive. The learning activities which are identified in Sections 4 to 10 are only examples of what might be done to support learning. Those who use this guide should therefore be selective when determining their *individual* priorities.

WORKING IN THE FOOD AND BEVERAGE SERVICE INDUSTRY

What is food and beverage service?

Food and beverage service is the essential link between the menu, beverages and other services on offer in an establishment, and the customers. You are the main point of contact between the customers and the establishment. Working in food and beverage service requires the blending of four things:

- product knowledge
- interpersonal skills
- technical skills
- team work

It is an important role in a noble profession, with increasing national and international status. Skills and knowledge, and therefore careers, are transferable between establishments, sectors and throughout the world.

Food can include a wide range of styles and cuisine types. These can be by country, such as traditional British or Italian, by type of cuisine such as oriental, or aiming for a speciality such as fish, vegetarian or health food.

Beverages include all alcoholic and non-alcoholic drinks. Alcoholic beverages include wines and all other types of alcoholic drink such as cocktails, beers and cider, spirits and liqueurs. Non-alcoholic beverages include bar beverages such as mineral waters, juices, squashes and aerated waters, as well as tea, coffee, chocolate, milk and milk drinks, and also proprietary drinks such as Bovril.

What types of operations are there?

Food and beverage service in its various forms can be found in a range of types of operations including restaurants, cafés, cafeterias, take-aways, canteens, function rooms, lounges and in-room service for hotel guests. There is a wide variety of sectors such as hotels, independent and chain restaurants, popular catering, pubs and wine bars, fast food, leisure attractions and banqueting. There are also sectors where food and beverages are provided as part of another business. These include transport catering, welfare, clubs, education, industrial feeding and the forces. In many cases the same type of operation, such as a table service restaurant, may be found in a wide variety of sectors.

For a detailed explanation of sectors read *Food and Beverage Service* Sections 1.1 to 1.4 and *The Beverage Book* Chapter 1.

What needs do customers have?

The reasons for eating out vary. It might be simply having to eat out because the person is unable to return home or because the person is celebrating some special occasion such as a birthday. However, the same people can have different needs at different times. In other words it is important to consider the needs people have rather than the type of people they are. This is because, for example, the business person during the week day can also be the family adult at the weekend, a conference delegate on another occasion or a traveller on the motorway.

For a detailed explanation of the meal experience and the needs people might have see *Food and Beverage Service* Section 1.5.

What types of food and beverage service are there?

Food and beverage service can be summarised under five main headings. These are:

1 Table service – where the customer is served at a laid table. This type of service, which includes, for instance, silver service or plated service, is found in most restaurants, cafés and in banqueting.

2 Self service – where the customer is required to help themselves from a buffet or counter. This type of service can be found in cafeterias and canteens.

3 Assisted service – where the customer is served part of the meal at a table and is required to obtain part through self-service from some form of display or buffet. This type of service is found in carvery-type operations and is often used for meals such as breakfast in hotels.

4 Single point service – where the customer orders, pays and receives the food and beverages, for instance at a counter, at a bar in licensed premises or at a vending machine.

5 Service in situ – where the food and drink is taken to where the customer is. This includes tray service in hospitals, trolley service, home delivery, lounge and room service.

For a detailed description of all service methods see *Food and Beverage Service* Section 1.6.

What are the range of jobs?

The range of operations and sectors above indicates that there is a wide variety of roles within food and beverage service. These roles range from waiters with differing levels of responsibility, lounge staff, room service staff, buffet and counter staff, bar staff, wine staff in restaurants, function catering staff and cashiers. However, most of the basic skills required are transferable to any type of operation. For example, carrying plates, trays, glasses and cutlery, and carving or beverage service skills are broadly similar wherever they are carried out. The variation is in the application of these skills, which is usually governed by the requirements of the particular establishment.

For a listing and explanation of the various jobs in food and beverage service read *Food and Beverage Service* Section 1.7 or *The Beverage Book* Chapter 1.

Are there any special legislative controls?

Yes. These include regulations on health, safety and hygiene, licensing laws which control the sale of alcoholic beverages and laws which govern the relationship between the customer and the business, including such aspects as the description of services and care for the customer's property. Hygiene in the handling and service of food items (beverages are counted as food) is critical to reduce risks to customers, and it is recommended that all service staff should at least have a Primary Hygiene Certificate.

For a more detailed explanation of these legislative requirements see *Food and Beverage Service* Section 10.1.

What about learning, training and qualifications?

If you are studying at a college you should be on a planned learning programme leading to a qualification. If you are working in the industry you should be receiving training, for your particular job, from your employer. However, in developing your skills, knowledge, general professionalism and your career, you also have considerable responsibility for your own learning.

This book, together with the other publications in the food and beverage service suite (*Food and Beverage Service 5th Edition* and *The Beverage Book*), is designed to assist you in developing your individual learning programme for your course or job requirements, your continuing development and in the recording of your progress and achievements.

Qualifications on offer

The Academy of Food and Wine Service
(0181 977 4419)
A professional association which offers flexible learning programmes in food service and wine service and the opportunity to achieve recognition by becoming a member of the Academy.

The City and Guilds of London Institute
(0171 294 2469)
A long-established awarding body for a wide range of qualifications, including National Vocational Qualifications, for all industries. Also awards the 7066, Certificate, Diploma and Advanced Diploma in Food and Beverage Service.

National Vocational Qualifications
These are available for food and beverage service through a number of awarding bodies. These include the Hospitality Training Foundation, City and Guilds of London Institute

and The Business and Technical Educational Council (BTEC). In most cases your employer will have to be registered as an assessment centre for you to obtain the qualifications. Courses for these qualifications are also available in colleges, which are approved as assessment centres, through both part- and full-time courses (see also page 12).

The Wine and Spirit Education Trust

(0171 236 3551)

A charitable trust supporting training and education in wines and spirits for the trade and the hotel and catering industry. The Trust offers a range of materials and courses leading to the Certificate, Higher Certificate and Diploma in Wines and Spirits. Those with at least five years' experience in the industry can apply to study for the prestigious Master of Wine award.

The Association of Wine Educators

(0181 995 2277)

This association can provide information about the range of short courses on offer.

In addition there are a variety of other study opportunities available at colleges which lead to other hospitality industry qualifications, such as the National and Higher Diplomas and degrees. There are also opportunities to study for the professional membership examinations of the Hotel and Catering, International Management Association.

Competitions

An additional way to measure and improve your ability is through entering competitions. For people working in food and beverage service these include:

The Académie Culinaire de France (UK)

(0181 874 8500)

Annual Awards of Excellence. These awards are available for people aged between 20 and 24 years, who are working in food and beverage service, as patissiers or chefs. It is an award for achieving a set standard, rather than being in a competition.

In addition there is the highly prestigious senior award, Meilleur Ouvrier de Grand Bretagne (MOGB). This is offered every four years for senior restaurant personnel, patissiers or chefs and is for people over the age of 26 years who are able to demonstrate the highest standards of craftsmanship. Again it is an award for achieving a set standard rather than being in a competition. Entry is by application.

The Academy of Food and Wine Service

(0181 977 4419)

Wine Waiter of the Year. This professional association runs this competition annually for those working as sommeliers. Entry is by application.

Hospitality Skills

(0181 977 4419)

Run every two years, usually at Hospitality Week in Birmingham, this competition is for people under the age of 22 years and offers the opportunity for a variety of awards up to Gold Medal in food and beverage service. This competition is also used to identify the UK entry for the International Youth Skill Olympics, held every two years. Entry is by nomination or application.

The Restaurateurs' Association of Great Britain

(0181 977 4419)

Young Waiter of the Year. This competition, which is run together with the Young Chef of the Year competition, is for people working in food and beverage service who are under the age of 25 years. It was the first competition in the UK for those working in food and beverage service. Entry is by application.

Salon Culinaire

The Salon Culinaire is held each year, alternately at Hotelympia in London and Hospitality Week in Birmingham (both Hotelympia and Hospitality Week are bi-annual exhibitions). As well as a wide range of cuisine based competitions the service competitions include the Cook and Serve and the Restaurant Sweet. The Cook and Serve is a joint entry for a chef and a waiter and the Restaurant Sweet is an individual entry to prepare (flambé) and serve a restaurant sweet dish. Entry is by application.

(Salon Director 01564 776 842)

The Savoy Education Trust

(0171 420 2310)

Food Service Award. This charitable trust, which supports a range of training and education initiatives across the industry, runs this competition on an annual basis. It is for those working in food and beverage service who are under the age of 25 years. Entry is by nomination or application.

USING THIS BOOK AND IDENTIFYING YOUR LEARNING NEEDS

Who should use this book?

This book has been designed to be used if you are currently studying or working in food and beverage service. It will help you prepare your personal learning programme for the development of your skills, knowledge and professionalism to meet the requirements of your course or current job (and your career). This book will also help you to develop a system to record your progress and learning achievement.

The book has been designed to be used in conjunction with two other books: *Food and Beverage Service* and *The Beverage Book*.

Food and Beverage Service provides a broad range of information about food and beverage service. It is a text book as well as a reference source. It will be relevant to you as an information source if you are studying or mainly working in food and beverage service and if, in addition, you are undertaking some study of, or have some responsibility for, alcoholic beverage service (for example wine service).

The Beverage Book is also a text book and reference source. It provides a more extensive coverage of beverage sales and service with substantial detail on alcoholic beverages, methods of production, descriptions and the wine growing regions. It will be particularly relevant if you have some main responsibility in alcoholic beverage service, for example as a wine waiter, or simply if you wish to develop a more in-depth knowledge of beverages generally.

This Section explains how to use this book and what else you will need to do to support your learning. Section 3 explains how to keep records of your progress and achievement and how these records may be used as evidence of meeting the assessment requirements for your achievement of NVQs.

How can this book be used?

You can use this book to support your learning and development in three main ways. These are:

Option 1
Read through Sections 1 to 3, set up your system for recording your progress as suggested in Section 3, and then work through Sections 4 to 10 in order. In effect the contents listing, on pages iii to v, becomes the structure for your learning.

Option 2
Read through Sections 1 to 3 and then assess your learning needs by completing the form (printed following page 12) after reading the notes on how to complete it, on page 13. This form, which has been designed so that it can be photocopied up to A4 size, then provides the structure for your learning programme.

Option 3

This is where you are registered for an NVQ. In this case you should follow the suggestion made in Option 2 above, but when completing the form printed after page 13 take care to also note the assessment requirements of the NVQ award you are seeking to achieve.

Whichever way you approach this book it will lead you to some or all of Sections 4 to 10. Each of these Sections starts with a short introduction which is followed by statements of what you should be able to do. There are then suggested learning activities which you are invited to undertake. There are six types of learning activity. These are:

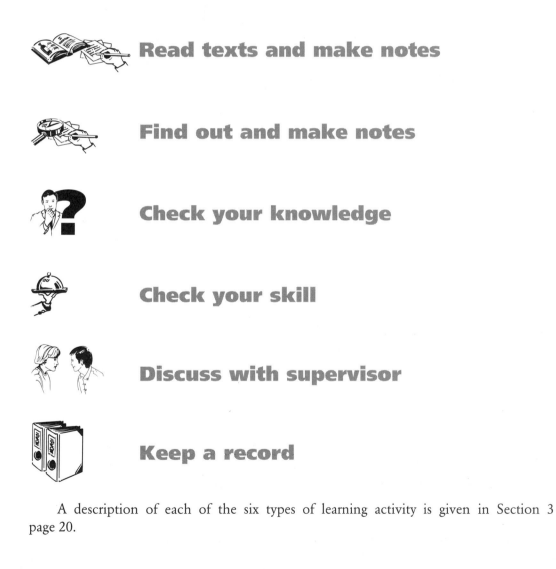

Read texts and make notes

Find out and make notes

Check your knowledge

Check your skill

Discuss with supervisor

Keep a record

A description of each of the six types of learning activity is given in Section 3 page 20.

What are NVQs?

The NVQs (including the Scottish SVQs) are qualifications which recognise what people are able to do in their jobs. They are based on industry standards (set out in separate units) which indicate what people are likely to need to be able to do, if they do the job well. NVQs are set at five Levels. This book is aimed at support learning and achievement equivalent to Levels 1 to 3 of the National Standards. The general definitions of the NVQ Levels 1 to 3 are:

Level 1 – Qualifications are for people whose work is mostly routine but involves a range of tasks and duties.

Level 2 – Qualifications are for people whose work is more varied, less routine and where this can be carried out well, on their own and as part of a team.

Level 3 – Qualifications are for people who supervise other staff at work. There are also qualifications which cover higher service skills.

What else do I need?

In undertaking this study programme you will benefit from the support of your supervisor/manager, who should be able to:

- give you support and encouragement in your learning and development
- provide you with feedback on your current performance and progress
- agree your achievements and sign these off

In order to ensure that you keep a record of your achievements, Section 3 also explains how to keep these records which may then be used as evidence to support your current or subsequent assessment for NVQs/SVQs.

How do I identify my learning needs?

If you are intending to use this book under Option 2 and 3 (as described on page 10) then the form printed after page 13 will help you to identify your learning needs. It also provides the basis for the structure of your learning programme. In order to use the form it can be photocopied from the book up to A4 size. It is advisable to file the form, when photocopied, into a two- or four-ring binder. It is clearly important to discuss this form with your tutor or supervisor, who will help and advise you in completing it.

Down the left-hand side of the form a range of food and beverage service tasks and duties is identified. At the top there are four key stages identified. These are:

Stage 1   Your job?

Here you should work through the form and mark with a tick, under this column, which of the tasks and duties you do in your current job (or in the case of students those which are required for your course).

Stage 2   Assess your needs

This stage asks three questions. The first two questions are about whether you are, or are not yet, competent. You should mark these in with a tick. The third question asks whether you are required to undertake the tasks and duties to meet the assessment requirements for a NVQ/SVQ award. In most cases it is likely that you will be doing the task or duty as part of your role, but this column allows for an identification of areas which you may not currently do but which you will need to do in order to meet the assessment requirements for an award. You can also use this third column if you are seeking to broaden your knowledge and skill beyond your current job or NVQ/SVQ award requirements.

Stage 3   Plan your learning

The first column identifies the page references in this book which are relevant to the task and duty in the left-hand column. The second column in this section is for you to identify your intended completion date for each of the areas you are going to undertake. This will then be your personal learning plan.

Stage 4   Record your achievement

In this last stage the first column is for you to record when you have completed the learning and are competent in the task/duty. The second column is for your tutor or supervisor's signature which will confirm that you have achieved the requirements.

It is important to stress that the records of achievement suggested in Section 3 of this book will be required as evidence to support the achievement of competence identified in the completed form. Without this supporting evidence the record will not be sufficient to be used as evidence to meet the assessment requirements for an NVQ/SVQ award.

[**Note:** to create an A4 size copy of the five page form printed after this page and the six individual record forms printed after page 21 of this book, first make a standard photocopy of each of the pages. With scissors or using a guillotine, trim these photocopies leaving about 1/3 cm around each of the forms. Then make another photocopy from each of the trimmed sheets, setting the photocopier print size to 125%. This set then becomes your master set. You can then make additional copies of your record forms from this set.]

Learning About Food & Beverage Service

FOOD AND BEVERAGE SERVICE
PERSONAL LEARNING PROGRAMME

Name _____

Job title _____

Department _____

Establishment _____

Manager/Supervisor _____

Tutor _____

Programme Start Date _____

TASKS AND DUTIES	YOUR JOB?	ASSESS YOUR NEEDS			PLAN YOUR LEARNING		RECORD YOUR ACHIEVEMENT	
	Check if part of your job?	Competent?	Not yet competent	Needed for qualification?	Work through this book pages	Planned completion	Competence achieved	Supervisor
Interpersonal Skills								
• Present a positive personal image to the customer					36–38			
• Balance the needs of the customer and the organisation								
• Respond to feelings expressed by the customer								
• Adapt methods of communication 　Deal with: 　adults 　children 　those with mobility difficulties 　those with communication difficulties 　customer complaints 　customer incidents								
Health, Safety and Security								
• Maintain personal health and hygiene					41, 42			
• Maintain a safe environment					42, 43			
• Maintain a secure environment 　report suspicious items 　report accidents					44, 45			
• Carry out procedures in the event of a fire					46, 47			

TASKS AND DUTIES	YOUR JOB?	ASSESS YOUR NEEDS			PLAN YOUR LEARNING		RECORD YOUR ACHIEVEMENT	
	Check if part of your job?	Competent?	Not yet competent	Needed for qualification?	Work through this book pages	Planned completion	Competence achieved	Supervisor
Service Areas, Equipment and Product Knowledge								
• Demonstrate knowledge of service areas					50, 51			
• Demonstrate knowledge and use of equipment					52–55			
• Develop and demonstrate product knowledge					56, 57			
Service Sequence								
• Establish and maintain working relationships					60–63			
• Take bookings					66, 67			
• Prepare service areas table service silver service carvery/buffet service					64, 65			
• Take orders for food and beverages and determine customer requirements					68–71			
• Serve food table service silver service carvery/buffet service					72, 73			
• Serve beverages non-alcoholic beverages wine other alcoholic beverages					74, 75			

TASKS AND DUTIES	YOUR JOB?	ASSESS YOUR NEEDS			PLAN YOUR LEARNING		RECORD YOUR ACHIEVEMENT	
	Check if part of your job?	Competent?	Not yet competent	Needed for qualification?	Work through this book pages	Planned completion	Competence achieved	Supervisor
• Clear during service					76, 77			
• Deal with payments					78, 79			
• Clear service areas after service					80, 81			
Specialised service skills								
• Provide specialised forms of service								
breakfast					84, 85			
afternoon teas					86, 87			
room service					88, 89			
lounge service					90, 91			
guéridon service					92, 93			
prepare, cook and serve food in a food service area								
Function Catering								
• Prepare for and serve at functions					96, 97			
• Contribute to function administration					98, 99			
• Contribute to function organisation					100, 101			
Supervisory Responsibilities								
• Supervise operation within licensing (and other) laws					104, 105			
• Contribute to the control of food and beverage operations					106, 107			

TASKS AND DUTIES	YOUR JOB?	ASSESS YOUR NEEDS			PLAN YOUR LEARNING		RECORD YOUR ACHIEVEMENT	
	Check if part of your job?	Competent?	Not yet competent	Needed for qualification?	Work through this book pages	Planned completion	Competence achieved	Supervisor
• Maintain cleaning programme in own area					108, 109			
• Maintain vending machine service					110, 111			
• Improve service reliability for customers					112, 113			
• Contribute to the development of teams and individuals					114, 115			
• Implement sales development activities					116, 117			

RECORDING YOUR LEARNING ACTIVITIES AND ACHIEVEMENTS

What is a portfolio?

A portfolio is a permanent record of your personal learning programme: your learning, progress, experience and achievement. It will be valuable to you when making applications for promotion or career development, as well as providing evidence of your achievement to meet the assessment requirements of the NVQ/SVQ.

It is suggested that you use a two- or four-ring binder which will first contain A4 size copies of the front page and the form, which is printed after page 13 of this book. This form records your current competence and the learning you are intending to undertake, allowing you to plan for this and identify when you have completed it to the satisfaction of your supervisor (or tutor). To support this there are six additional record forms, one for each of the six learning activities of this book. These forms will record the particular learning activities you have undertaken and the results you have achieved.

Your portfolio may also contain your job description, information about the establishment in which you work, and details of procedures and instructions relevant to working in your establishment.

What are the learning activities and how do I record my learning and achievements?

Sections 4 to 10 all contain a brief introduction, followed by a number of statements indicating what you should be able to do in undertaking the tasks or duties being discussed. These statements are then followed, in each section, by a range of suggested learning activities. These are all based on six learning activities.

For each of these activities there is a form which can be used to record your progress. The blanks of these forms appear after page 21. These forms may be photocopied up to A4 for inclusion in your ring binder (see note on page 13). For each of the forms there is a page giving guidance on how to complete it. Whenever you are undertaking one of the six learning activities you should complete one or more of these forms.

The six learning activities and the use of the activity record form are described below:

 **Read texts and make notes**

Here you will be asked to read Chapters, Sections or pages from either *Food and Beverage Service* or *The Beverage Book*. When reading you will have been asked to make notes on aspects which relate to your course or job requirements. The form for this activity allows you to record a note of what Chapters or Sections you have read and the notes you have obtained.

Find out and make notes

Here you will be asked to investigate specific requirements, procedures or systems at your own establishment and to keep a record of your findings. The form will allow you to record what you have investigated and the results you have obtained. You may also include behind this form copies of procedures or internal regulations.

 ## Check your knowledge

Here you will be asked to assess your knowledge of a particular aspect. You can do this by being questioned by your supervisor or colleagues or by being observed while you are undertaking a particular task (such as your supervisor assessing your product knowledge through observing you taking an order from a party of guests). The form will enable you to record the knowledge aspects you have checked, and how and when this was done.

Check your skill

This is similar to checking your knowledge, but here you are being asked to assess your skills, which could be technical or interpersonal. The methods of assessment could be similar to those suggested for checking your knowledge.

 ## Discuss with supervisor

Here you will be asked to discuss with your supervisor (or tutor) a particular aspect of your job (or course) requirements. This may be to discuss your progress, enable you to undertake some activity outside of your normal job or where you want to clarify your understanding of the establishment's policy on a particular aspect of service. The record form enables you to make a note of these discussions and the outcome.

 ## Keep a record

Here you will have been asked to record particular events or occasions when you have completed particular tasks. This might include, for example, a record of your service at a special function or private party, or dealing with an unusual request, handling a situation which is out of the ordinary or where you have received additional recognition or praise for your work.

Learning About Food & Beverage Service – Section _____

NOTES FROM READING

PERSONAL LEARNING RECORD OF _____

SHEET NO _____

DATE	TOPIC/SUBJECT	REFERENCES	NOTES MADE ON	FURTHER READING	ACTION POINTS

Learning About Food & Beverage Service – Section

Write here the number and title of the section you are working on

SHEET NO _____

NOTES FROM READING

PERSONAL LEARNING RECORD OF _____

DATE	TOPIC/SUBJECT	REFERENCES	NOTES MADE ON	FURTHER READING	ACTION POINTS
Put here the date or dates when you undertook the reading.	_List here what you are reading about. For example attributes of food service personnel or tea and coffee service._	_Give the reference of the sources of information you are using. Use abbreviations such as, for example, FBS CH10 could mean Food and Beverage Service Chapter 10._	_List here what you have made notes on. Your notes should then be put together with this form in your folder._	_List here areas where you feel you may need to find some further information, either in the two main texts or in other texts or information sources._	_Indentify here any action you are to carry out as a result of undertaking the learning activity. This could be for instance discussing your progress with your supervisor or other colleagues._

Learning About Food & Beverage Service – Section _____

NOTES FROM FINDING OUT

PERSONAL LEARNING RECORD OF _____

DATE	TOPIC/SUBJECT	INFORMATION SOURCES	NOTES MADE ON/ INFORMATION OBTAINED ON	FURTHER INFORMATION REQUIRED	ACTION POINTS

Learning About Food & Beverage Service – Section

NOTES FROM FINDING OUT

Write here the number and title of the section you are working on

SHEET NO _____

PERSONAL LEARNING RECORD OF _____

DATE	TOPIC/SUBJECT	INFORMATION SOURCES	NOTES MADE ON / INFORMATION OBTAINED ON	FURTHER INFORMATION REQUIRED	ACTION POINTS
Put here the date or dates when you undertook your investigation.	_List here what you are finding out about. For example your establishment procedure for reporting sickness or the location of fire exits._	_List here the sources of information you have obtained. This could include published information in your establishment such as staff handbooks and notices or other staff._	_List here what you have made notes on. These notes could then be put together with any printed information you have obtained (such as a copy of the wine list) with this form in your folder._	_List here areas where you feel you may need to find some further information._	_Indentify here any action you are to carry out as a result of undertaking your investigation. This could include checking the information you have with other departments._

Learning About Food & Beverage Service – Section _____

NOTES ON KNOWLEDGE

PERSONAL LEARNING RECORD OF _____

SHEET NO ____

DATE	TOPIC/SUBJECT	CHECKED WITH	SATISFACTORY ASPECTS	ASPECTS REQUIRING FURTHER WORK	ACTION POINTS

Learning About Food & Beverage Service – Section _____

Write here the number and title of the section you are working on

NOTES ON KNOWLEDGE

SHEET NO _____

PERSONAL LEARNING RECORD OF _____

DATE	TOPIC/SUBJECT	CHECKED WITH	SATISFACTORY ASPECTS	ASPECTS REQUIRING FURTHER WORK	ACTION POINTS
Put here the date or dates when you checked your knowledge.	List here what you are checking your knowledge on. For example lay-up requirements, accompaniments or menu items.	List here who you have checked your knowledge with. This could be your colleagues or your supervisor.	List here those aspects where your knowledge is satisfactory. The column on the right here is for your supervisor or tutor to initial if you have checked your knowledge with them. Your supervisor or tutor may also like to add their own comments to this form as a record.	List here those areas of knowledge where you will need to continue to study or where you feel you may need to find some further information.	Identify here any action you are to carry out as a result of checking your knowledge. This could be for instance arranging a date for a follow up.

This page is photocopiable © Cousins and Smith, published by Hodder and Stoughton 1998

Learning About Food & Beverage Service - Section _____

NOTES ON SKILLS

PERSONAL LEARNING RECORD OF _____

SHEET NO ____

DATE	TOPIC/SUBJECT	CHECKED WITH	COMPETENT IN	FURTHER TRAINING PRACTICE REQUIRED	ACTION POINTS

Learning About Food & Beverage Service – Section

Write here the number and title of the section you are working on _____

NOTES ON SKILLS

SHEET NO _____

PERSONAL LEARNING RECORD OF _____

DATE	TOPIC/SUBJECT	CHECKED WITH	COMPETENT IN	FURTHER TRAINING PRACTICE REQUIRED	ACTION POINTS
Put here the date or dates when you checked your skills.	List here which of your skills you are seeking to assess. For example clearing skills, or dealing with a complaint.	List here who you have checked your skills with. This could be your colleagues or your supervisor.	List here those aspects where your skills are satisfactory. The column on the right here is for your supervisor or tutor to initial if you have checked your skills with them. Your supervisor or tutor may also like to add their own comments to this form as a record.	List here your skill areas where you feel you may need some further training or practice.	Identify here any action you are to carry out as a result of checking your skills. This could be for instance setting a new date to check certain skills again.

This page is photocopiable © Cousins and Smith, published by Hodder and Stoughton 1998

Learning About Food & Beverage Service - Section _____

NOTES OF SUPERVISOR DISCUSSION

PERSONAL LEARNING RECORD OF _____

SHEET NO _____

DATE	TOPIC/SUBJECT	PURPOSE OF DISCUSSION	OUTCOME OF DISCUSSION	ACTION POINTS

Learning About Food & Beverage Service – Section

NOTES OF SUPERVISOR DISCUSSION

PERSONAL LEARNING RECORD OF _____

Write here the number and title of the section you are working on

SHEET NO _____

DATE	TOPIC/SUBJECT	PURPOSE OF DISCUSSION	OUTCOME OF DISCUSSION	ACTION POINTS
Put here the date or dates when you had the discussion with your supervisor/ tutor.	*List here what you are to discuss with your supervisor. For example procedures for a fire drill or the role and responsibilities of service personnel in other food service areas.*	*Identify here what you are seeking to gain from the discussion with your supervisor. This could range from, for instance, seeking clarification on some aspect of your establishments procedures or discussing your progress in your training and learning programme.*	*Identify here the result of your discussion. This follows from reflecting on the purpose you have identified and the extent to which the purpose has been achieved.*	*Identify here any action you are to carry out as a result of having the discussion. This could be for instance making the arrangements for further training or arrange a further meeting with your supervisor/ tutor.*

Learning About Food & Beverage Service - Section

NOTES FOR RECORD

PERSONAL LEARNING RECORD OF _____

SHEET NO _____

DATE	TOPIC/SUBJECT	SERVICE PERIOD	DESCRIPTION	WHO INVOLVED	ACTION POINTS

Learning About Food & Beverage Service – Section

NOTES FOR RECORD

PERSONAL LEARNING RECORD OF _____

DATE	TOPIC/SUBJECT	SERVICE PERIOD	DESCRIPTION	WHO INVOLVED	ACTION POINTS
Put here the date or dates when you completed this record.	*List here what you are recording. This could be a particular event or occasion when you have completed specific tasks. For example service of a special function, dealing with an unusual request.*	*Identify here the service period e.g. luncheon or dinner. This could also be for instance special luncheon party or a wedding breakfast for 100.*	*Give a brief description of what you undertook.*	*Identify here who else was involved. This refers to both your colleagues and to the customers e.g. a family with children. The column on the right is for your supervisor or tutor to initial to confirm what you have undertaken. Your supervisor or tutor may also like to add his/her own comments to this form.*	*Identify here any action you are to carry out as a result of undertaking the learning activity. This could be for instance arranging to undertake this activity again to improve your experience and develop your confidence.*

APPRECIATING CUSTOMER NEEDS

Appreciating customer needs

Food and beverage establishments are primarily designed to meet a range of customer needs. The needs customers have are varied and not all the needs may be satisfied by a particular operation. From a server's point of view it is important to have an appreciation of customer needs and the extent to which any of these are likely to be satisfied by the establishment's food, beverages, level of service and other services. In this way you will be able to make a contribution to the minimisation of conflicts, as you will be aware of when potential difficulties may arise and the establishment's procedures for dealing with them.

Appreciating customer needs means that you should be able to:

- ❖ identify the range of needs your customers are wanting to satisfy
- ❖ demonstrate your knowledge of the range of services offered by your establishment
- ❖ respond to the needs of customers
- ❖ endeavour to minimise conflict between customer and your establishment needs
- ❖ follow the procedures and routines for dealing with complaints

Learning activities

Read *Food and Beverage Service* Sections 1.1 to 1.6 and 10.4. Make notes on:
- the range of needs customers are wanting to satisfy, generally
- the type of establishment (for example sector, type of service) you work in

Consider your own establishment and identify specifically:
- the range of customers currently using the establishment and identify their likely needs
- changes which may take place in the range of customers, depending on the day, time of day or season
- changes which may take place in the needs customers have depending on the day, time of day or season

Consider your own establishment and:
- draw up a profile of the establishment by describing the range of services offered

Compare the profile of your own establishment with notes you have written about the range of customers and the different needs they may be wishing to satisfy, and then:
- identify where your establishment is likely to meet the needs of the range of customers
- identify where these needs might not be met

Discuss the range of customers and the differing needs they might have with your supervisor or colleagues. Make notes on:
- the extent to which your analysis was accurate
- additional aspects (if necessary) that you should now take into account following your discussion

Ask your supervisor to discuss with you the range of findings you have and note:
- areas where you are in line with what the establishment is expecting you to achieve
- any differences you have with your supervisor, identifying why you may have these different perspectives

Identify with your supervisor the procedures and routines for dealing with:
- conflict between the needs of the customer and the requirements of the establishment
- customer complaints

Read the Section of this book concerned with developing interpersonal skills (pages 60 to 63) and follow the learning activities proposed there.

Either through role play or being observed, explain the range of services offered by the establishment in relation to different types of customers. Identify areas where you are:
- able to carry out this task
- areas where you need to consider more practise

Ask your supervisor to discuss your progress with you. Note:
● areas where you are both satisfied with your performance
● areas where you need to continue to develop your knowledge and skill

When you are working keep a regular note on:
● the range of customers you are serving and how their needs compare
● needs which are new to you and how you have responded to them
● times when there has been conflict between the needs of the customer and the establishment and how you have contributed to minimising these
● times when you have dealt with customer complaints and the extent to which this has been successful

HEALTH, SAFETY AND SECURITY

Maintaining personal health and hygiene

Employers and staff are obliged to maintain high standards of health and safety. Particular attention should be paid to your appearance and in maintaining hygienic working practices. Plenty of rest and a healthy diet will assist you in ensuring a high standard of personal grooming.

Maintaining your personal health and hygiene means that you should be able to:

- ❖ wear clean, smart and appropriate clothing, footwear and headgear
- ❖ maintain high standards of personal grooming
- ❖ ensure that cuts, grazes and wounds are treated properly
- ❖ report illnesses and infections
- ❖ demonstrate hygienic and safe working practices
- ❖ ensure work is carried out in line with both legal *and* your establishment requirements

Learning activities

Read *Food and Beverage Service* Section 1.8 about a professional and hygienic appearance. Make a list of:
- the factors which contribute to developing high standards of personal hygiene
- factors which contribute to developing high standards of personal appearance

Consider your own establishment and determine the policy on:
- requirement for uniform
- restrictions on jewellery
- restriction on perfume, after shave and cosmetics
- what legislation applies to personal health and hygiene
- where such information can be found from both within the establishment and externally
- what the disciplinary procedure is for staff who do not meet health and hygiene standards
- the location of first aid boxes
- procedures to be followed for reporting illnesses and infections
- procedures to be followed in respect of cuts and grazes and other wounds

Together with your colleagues or supervisor discuss:
- why it is important to comply with health and safety legislation
- the possible effects of not maintaining good personal health and hygiene
- ways in which you feel hygiene practices can be improved within your establishment
- establishment procedures for health and hygiene
- areas where you need to undertake some further learning

Through being observed by your supervisor whilst working, assess your ability in:
- meeting the uniform requirements of your establishment
- maintaining high standards of personal grooming
- dealing properly with cuts, grazes and wounds
- reporting illnessess and infections
- demonstrating hygienic and safe working practices
- working within legal and other requirements of your establishment

Review your personal health and hygiene with your supervisor and make notes on:
- the extent to which you meet the establishment requirements in personal health and hygiene
- how improvements can be made to hygienic practices

Keep records of any instances when you have:
- completed an accident form
- taken action as a result of customer or colleague feedback on hygiene and appearance
- fulfilled establishment requirements on health and hygiene matters

Maintain a safe environment

Employers and staff are obliged to maintain a safe environment for staff, customers and lawful visitors

In contributing to the maintenance of a safe environment, you should be able to:

❖ contribute to the safety and security of customers, staff and visitors

❖ operate within the safety and security requirements of your establishment

❖ identify and report potential hazards

❖ report accidents

Learning activities

Read *Food and Beverage Service* Section 10.1 on maintaining a safe environment and make notes on:

● any potential safety hazards you can identify in both public and staff working areas

● the precautions you can take to advise customers, staff and visitors of these potential hazards, to ensure that they do not become real hazards

Find out about your company policy on the following safety matters including:

● how customers are warned of hazards or potential hazards

● how inspecting and risk assessment is carried out to ensure safety at all times

● how often inspection and assessment is carried out

● dealing with aggressive, violent, drunk, ill and drug-affected customers

● establishment procedure for reporting hazards

Together with your colleagues or supervisor discuss:

● why it is important to comply with safety legislation

● what are the possible effects of *not* maintaining a safe environment

● ways in which you feel safety can be improved within your establishment

● your establishment procedures for safety

- your responsibilities in respect of safety
- areas where you need to undertake some further learning

Through being observed by your supervisor whilst working, assess your ability in:

- contributing to the safety and security of customers, staff and visitors
- working within the safety and security requirements of your establishment
- reporting hazards
- reporting accidents

With your supervisor review:

- the extent to which you are meeting the establishment requirements for the maintenance of a safe environment
- areas where your knowledge is as required
- areas where you will need to undertake further learning

While you are working keep a record of:

- any instances where you have completed equipment fault reports, the incident or accident book, or taken action as a result of customer feedback on safety matters
- any instances where you have identified safety issues and what you have done about them

Maintain a secure environment

Security covers many areas, but essentially evolves around buildings, belongings and people. You will find varying degrees of security depending on where you work. For example, if you work in an airport or city centre location, or have particular types of clientele, it is likely that security measures will be higher here than in a small, suburban establishment. Wherever you work, security safeguards people – so it is in everyone's interest to be vigilant and mindful of security matters at all times.

In contributing to the maintenance of a secure environment, you should be able to:

❖ ensure the security of unauthorised areas

❖ operate the establishment policy on suspicious individuals

❖ act upon the discovery of a suspicious item

❖ report lost property

Learning activities

Read *Food and Beverage Service* Section 10.1 on maintaining a secure environment. Make a list of
- the security checks you feel need to be made within your premises
- how often these checks should be made

With the establishment in which you work in mind, make notes on:
- areas which are considered to be low-risk security areas
- medium-risk security areas
- high-risk security areas
- the reasons for the security designation of areas
- the procedures used when carrying out an inspection
- the establishment policy on restricted access areas, suspicious people or items
- the procedure for dealing with lost items

Together with your colleagues or your supervisor discuss:
- the procedures for the inspection of your premises
- the various routines which should be followed in dealing with security matters
- the extent to which you are fully conversant with security matters

● areas where you need to undertake some further learning

Under the supervision of the person in charge of security:
● perform a security inspection within your establishment

Discuss with your supervisor your contribution the maintenance of a secure environment, and make notes on:
● the extent to which you are conversant with the establishment regulations for security matters
● the extent to which you are fulfilling the requirements placed upon you for security matters
● areas where you need to undertake further learning

While at work keep a record of:
● any incidents which have involved you in undertaking security procedures

Carry out procedures in the event of a fire

Periodic fire drills are part of our everyday lives. This training must be taken seriously, for in the event of a real fire people's lives as well as your own may depend on *your* actions. Tackling fires can be dangerous and is not generally encouraged, however it is as well to know how to use fire-fighting equipment as it can be crucial in preventing a small fire becoming a catastrophe.

In assisting in fire safety you should be able to:

❖ state the fire procedures for your establishment
❖ carry out the establishment procedures in the event of a fire

Learning activities

Read *Food and Beverage Service* Section 10.1 on identifying fire extinguishers and:
● note the contents of each extinguisher
● note the types of fire each extinguisher can be used on

For your establishment gather information and make notes on:
● the fire procedures required
● the location of fire exits, extinguishers and assembly points
● your responsibilities in the event of a fire

Together with your colleagues or supervisor discuss and make notes on:
● your identification of the location of the fire extinguishers
● the identification and uses of the various fire extinguishers
● the procedures to be followed in the event of a fire
● your responsibilities in the procedure
● the special needs of customers and staff
● areas where you may need some further training

Through being observed by your supervisor or fire officer, whilst undertaking a fire drill, assess your ability in:
● fulfilling the establishment procedures in the event of a fire

Discuss with your supervisor your contribution to the fire safety of your establishment, and on:

- the extent to which you know and can demonstrate your understanding of the fire procedures
- areas where you both agree you are competent
- areas where you may need to undertake some further learning

During your time at work keep a record of:

- any training you receive
- any time you are involved in a fire drill
- any incident during which you have had to follow the procedures
- any special circumstances you have had to deal with
- any difficulties you have been faced with and how you have overcome these

SERVICE AREAS, EQUIPMENT AND PRODUCT KNOWLEDGE

Finding your way around service areas

Your establishment consists of a variety of work areas. These areas fit together like the pieces of a jigsaw, making up the overall operation. Some areas may be independent of the rest, while some may be a sub-section of another area: For example, the bar area may be separated from a restaurant area or may be integral to it. To enable you to work efficiently as a team member, it is important that you know the function of the areas, the contribution they make to the service, and the roles of the staff within them.

For service areas you should be able to:

❖ explain the layout of all service areas which you use or work with

❖ know the purpose of the various service areas

❖ identify the roles of the staff working in and responsible for these areas

Learning activities

Read *Food and Beverage Service* Sections 2.1 to 2.8 and make notes on:
- the main back of house areas in your establishment

Sketch a plan of the layout of each of the service areas within your own establishment and make notes on:
- the main purpose of the area
- how this work contributes to the service
- the roles of the staff within each area
- how you are expected to liaise with each of the areas
- the location of fire and emergency exits, fire extinguishers and access for the disabled, if appropriate

With your colleagues or supervisor discuss:
- the purpose of each of the service areas
- the roles of staff within the service areas
- the communications requirements for the establishment and how this contributes to the service
- good liaison between the various areas

For each of the service areas produce notes on:

● the liaison requirements between the various areas and your work area
● the requirements placed on you as being part of the process
● how this actually works in practice

Through being observed by your supervisor whilst working, assess your ability in:

● explaining the layout and purpose of the service areas to a colleague
● working appropriately within the service areas and respecting the roles of staff working in, and those responsible for, the various service areas

Discuss your sketch, notes and reports with your supervisor to identify:

● the extent to which your understanding of the operations is accurate
● the extent to which your contribution is in line with the establishment procedures
● additional aspects where you may need to undertake further investigation

When appropriate keep a record of:

● your contribution to the development of efficient liaison between the various areas
● difficulties you have come across and how you have dealt with them

Using equipment

The equipment you use may help to make your job easier or enhance the standard of the service. When properly maintained this equipment will give you years of service, so it is important to know how to look after it. Some equipment may have special limitations of use or health and safety requirements which must be considered

In using any equipment in your establishment you should be able to:

❖ identify and state the use of all equipment which you are expected to use
❖ explain the limitations of equipment use and identify who is able to use the equipment
❖ demonstrate your ability in basic technical skills
❖ apply required precautions in the use of equipment
❖ demonstrate safe and hygienic working practices in the use of equipment

Learning activities

Make a list of all the equipment you use:
- when preparing for service
- during service
- when taking payment
- after service

Read *Food and Beverage Service* Sections 2.10 to 2.15 and make notes on the equipment you use as part of your job, including:
- types of seating within your establishment
- sizes and shapes of tables
- type and sizes of linen or disposables
- make and type of crockery
- type of tableware used and its finish
- types and sizes of glassware
- any other equipment used

Discuss with your supervisor and make notes on:
- any equipment which you have listed where you do not know its use or how to use it
- equipment which you must use under supervision

- equipment which you must be trained to use
- any equipment which may be used in substitution for the correct item
- equipment which should not be used for alternative purposes

With reference to your own establishment find out about and make notes on:
- your responsibilities for the care and maintenance of equipment
- requirements for the security of equipment
- the location of instructions for use of equipment
- procedures for reporting faults and shortages

Read *Food and Beverage Service* Section 5.1 and make notes on:
- the techniques you should be able to demonstrate for each of the six basic technical skills
- activities you need to undertake to achieve competence

Find out and make notes on:
- which of the six basic technical skills (see above) you are required to use in your establishment
- the specific requirements of your establishment in the use of these skills

Through discussion with your supervisor or colleagues check your knowledge of:
- the different tasks you are required to carry out and the way in which you should use your technical skills

Having practised your skills ask your supervisor or colleagues to observe you while working, in order to:
- evaluate your competence in the application of the basic technical skills
- identify areas where you have achieved competence
- record areas where you require more training and/or practice

Discuss your abilities in the application of skills with your supervisor and record:
- skills where you both agree you are already competent
- areas where you both agree you require more practice/training

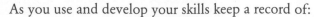

As you use and develop your skills keep a record of:
- the range of tasks where you have applied the various technical skills
- the improvement in your technical ability over time
- the improvement in your working methods and efficiency, as a result of increasing ability and confidence in the range of skills

With your supervisor or colleagues discuss:
- the use of equipment
- restrictions on the use of equipment
- areas where you may need to undertake further training or more reading

Find out and make notes on safety and hygiene practices when using equipment for:
- housekeeping duties
- preparation for service
- during service
- following service

While at work ask your supervisor or colleagues to observe you to check on your:
- correct use of cutlery, tableware and glassware during service in the restaurant
- correct use of equipment in the still room
- attention to health and safety issues when using any equipment

Arrange to discuss with your supervisor a review of your skills and knowledge in using equipment. Make notes on:
- the extent to which you are meeting the establishment requirements in the use of the equipment
- a review of the equipment currently being used and possible alternatives
- aspects of your skill and knowledge where you both feel that some further training or study would be appropriate

When convenient while at work, keep a note on:
- the range of equipment that you have used
- the ease of use of the equipment

- contributions you have made to cleaning and maintenance of equipment
- contributions you have made to the maintenance of stocks of equipment

Developing your product knowledge

Along with technical skills, interpersonal skills and the ability to work as part of a team, product knowledge is a key requirement for working in food and beverage service. Having a good knowledge of the food and drink items on offer improves your confidence and increases your ability to inform customers. Extending your study will further increase your knowledge and therefore your confidence, as well as increasing your appreciation of food and beverages generally.

Having the appropriate product knowledge means that you should be able to:

❖ demonstrate your knowledge of all the menu items, and alcoholic and non-alcoholic beverages, which are on offer in your establishment

❖ demonstrate your ability in the correct service requirements of all food and beverage items

❖ advise customers of the limitations on customisation of menu and beverage items which may be offered

❖ provide information to customers with special dietary needs

❖ advise customers on the matching of food and drinks

Learning activities

Using copies of the menus for your establishment:
● note the ingredients, cooking methods and service requirements for each item

To help you appreciate that there are a number of ways of both making dishes and serving them, read *Food and Beverage Service* Chapter 3 and:
● use the information to extend your knowledge of the menu items on offer
● determine where there are differences between the published information and your establishment

Using copies of the beverage list of your establishment:
● note the ingredients and service requirements of each item

To help you appreciate the breadth of the possible beverage items and service methods, comparing this with the extent to which these are offered by your establishment, read *Food and Beverage Service* Chapter 4 and Sections 5.8 and 5.9 or *The Beverage Book* Chapters 3 to 6 and 11 and:
- use the information to extend your knowledge of the beverage items on offer
- determine where there are differences between the published information and your establishment

In discussion with your colleagues and your supervisor determine and make notes on:
- menu and beverage items which require you to seek further information from the customer (for example cooking steaks)
- menu and beverage items which may be offered in alternative ways (for example menu items without sauces or drink items with or without ice)
- note where there would be extra charges for the provision of these menu or beverage items

In order to develop your appreciation of special diets read *Food and Beverage Service* Section 3.1 and:
- make notes on the special needs customers might have

In order to be able to inform those with special dietary requirements:
- use the notes on the menu and beverage items you already have and identify items offered by your establishment where you may have to seek further information

In order to develop your knowledge of food and wine harmony read *Food and Beverage Service* Section 4.10 or *The Beverage Book* Chapter 10 and:
- using the notes you already have identify for each menu item appropriate alcoholic and non-alcoholic beverages which might be recommended to the customer

Check with your supervisor the establishment policies and procedures on:
- variations to the menu and food items and beverage items
- providing information to those with special dietary needs

With your supervisor and/or colleagues discuss your knowledge of:
- the food items on the menu and their service requirements
- the beverage items on offer and their service requirements
- food and wine harmony recommendations
- food and beverage items on offer which would be suitable to meet the needs of those with special diets

Make notes on those areas where your knowledge is in line with the needs of customers and the establishment, and those areas where you will need to undertake further investigation.

Through being observed by your supervisor or colleagues whilst working check your skills in:
- describing all menu and beverage items on offer
- the service of food and beverage items
- advising customers of the limitations on customisation of menu and beverage items
- providing information to customers with special dietary needs
- advising customers on the matching of food and drinks

When you are working keep a periodic note of:
- the range of dishes and beverages which you serve regularly and those which you serve only sometimes
- any special requests which you have dealt with and how these were dealt with
- times when you have been asked to make particular recommendations to customers on food and beverage items

DEVELOPING SERVICE SKILLS

Developing interpersonal skills

Interpersonal skills are about the way you communicate, anticipate and react to customer needs. These skills will help to shape the customers' impression of the standards and quality of the service they can expect to receive at your establishment.

In applying interpersonal skills you should be able to:

❖ maintain a professional attitude towards colleagues and customers

❖ contribute to the development of team work within the food and beverage area(s)

❖ address customers according to the establishment policies/procedures

❖ deal with customer enquiries, having sufficient knowledge of the menu, beverages, service requirements, and the other services offered by your establishment

❖ operate under the establishment routines for dealing with complaints, accidents, special requests and the policies on the provision of services

❖ adapt methods of communication suited to customers with special needs

❖ use opportunities to identify and discuss work-related matters

Learning activities

Go to Sections 4 and 6 (pages 56 to 58) of this book (either now or later) and identify:

● activities you will need to undertake to ensure you are fully conversant with the range of customer needs

● activities you will need to undertake to ensure you have sufficient knowledge of the menu, beverages and other service offered by your establishment

Read *Food and Beverage Service* Section 1.7 or *The Beverage Book* Chapter 1 on food and beverage personnel and make notes on:

● the staffing structure of your establishment

● the titles of various staff in your establishment

For your own establishment make notes on the policy for:

● greeting customers

● addressing customers

● attention to customers during their meal

● procedure when customers depart

Read *Food and Beverage Service* Section 5.2 or *The Beverage Book* Chapter 11 and make notes on:

- the opportunities for you to demonstrate your interpersonal skills
- – with your colleagues
  - on greeting customers
  - during service
  - for customers with special needs
  - on the departure of customers

Through discussion with your supervisor or colleagues check your knowledge of:

- the different tasks you are required to carry out and the ways in which you should use your interpersonal skills

Having practised your skills ask your supervisor or colleagues to observe you while at work in order to:

- evaluate your competence in the application of your interpersonal skills, especially in the meeting of establishment requirements and in your body language, eye contact and listening skills
- identify areas where you have achieved competence
- record areas where you require more training and/or practice

Discuss your abilities in the application of skills with your supervisor and record:

- skills where you both agree that you are already competent
- areas where you both agree you require more practice/training

As you use and develop your interpersonal skills, keep a record of:

- the range of tasks where you have applied the various technical skills
- the improvement in your interpersonal skills over time
- the improvement in your working relationships, and your dealing with a range of customer as a result of your increasing ability and confidence in the application of your interpersonal skills

Discuss your individual effort as a team member with your supervisor and record:

- your strengths
- your weaknesses
- ways in which you can work together to improve your performance

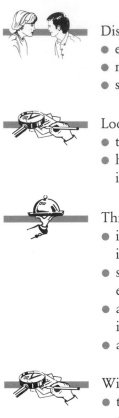

Discuss team work with your supervisor and list ways of:
- encouraging teamwork
- monitoring teamwork
- solving teamwork-related problems

Look at the duties of staff in your section and make notes on:
- the way they work as a team
- how teamwork could be improved through the application of interpersonal skills

Through being observed by your supervisor or colleagues while at work:
- identify situations where your application of interpersonal skills is appropriate
- situations where you are meeting with the requirements of your establishment
- areas where you are competent in the use and application of interpersonal skills
- areas where you will need to undertake further practice

With regard to your own establishment make notes on:
- the most common customer complaints you receive in your establishment
- the procedures for dealing with these complaints effectively
- how the complaint should be recorded
- how these complaints can be utilised in a positive way

Keep records of complaints you have dealt with and make notes on:
- complaints you have dealt with face to face, on the phone, or through the post
- how complaints have been dealt with and if a satisfactory conclusion was reached

With regard to your own establishment make notes on:
- the procedures to be followed in the event of an accident

In discussion with your colleagues or supervisor establish:
- the extent to which you know the procedures to be followed when an accident occurs
- aspects where you will need to seek further information or clarification

Read *Food and Beverage Service* Section 5.2 and make notes on the requirements of those with special needs for:
● mobility
● sight
● communication

Through being observed by your colleagues or supervisor while at work:
● test your interpersonal skills at dealing with special needs customers
● identify those areas where you are competent
● identify those areas where you need to do further work

Arrange to review your application of interpersonal skills with your supervisor, in order to:
● establish those areas where you are both happy about your use of appropriate skills
● those areas where you are fully working within the requirements of the establishment
● those areas where you would like more guidance
● those areas where you will need to undertake further work

Whilst working keep a record of:
● any accident you have had to deal with
● special requests which have been made to you and how you have dealt with these
● the range of customers with special needs you have dealt with and how successful you have been in dealing with them

Preparation for service

Preparing for service or *mise-en-place* ('put in place') as it is often called, is essential to the smooth and efficient operation of the service area during service. Each establishment will have its own routines and procedures to ensure that the preparation meets the standard expected.

In contributing to the preparation for service you should be able to:

❖ carry out a variety of preparatory tasks and duties within the food and beverage service area

❖ observe health and safety requirements

❖ operate within the requirements of the establishment

Learning activities

Review Sections 4 to 6 of this book and make notes on:

● any additional learning you will need to undertake to support your achievement in preparing for service

Read *Food and Beverage Service* Section 5.4 or *The Beverage Book* Chapter 11 and:

● list the various preparatory duties that may need to be undertaken in a food service area

For your establishment make notes on:

● the full range of preparatory duties required

● your specific responsibilities in undertaking these activities

● the procedures and systems to be observed when undertaking preparatory tasks

● how these tasks are being assessed to ensure they meet the requirements of the establishment

● how stock levels of items such as cutlery, glassware, paper, linen and so on are determined

● the procedure for ordering replacement stock

● the range of layouts of the dining areas which may be expected, for example for special parties

Together with your colleagues or your supervisor check your knowledge of the preparatory tasks and make notes on:

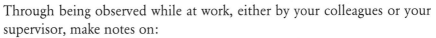

- the extent to which you know about all the preparatory tasks required
- the extent to which you are able to describe your contribution to the preparation requirements
- areas where you are confident in your knowledge of the requirements
- areas where you will need to undertake further work

Through being observed while at work, either by your colleagues or your supervisor, make notes on:

- your ability to carry out the preparatory tasks expected of you
- those areas where you are meeting the requirements of the establishment
- those areas where you still have additional learning or practice to undertake

Together with a colleague or your supervisor carry out a pre-service check for your service area and make notes on:

- those areas where you have met the establishment requirements
- those areas where you have not met the requirements
- aspects of the preparation which have been affected by things outside your control
- how you intend to follow these aspects up
- areas where you will need to undertake further practice or training

Arrange to review your contribution to preparatory tasks with your supervisor, in order to:

- establish those areas where you are both happy about your contribution
- those areas where you are fully working within the requirements of the establishment
- those areas where you would like more guidance
- those areas where you will need to undertake further work

During working times keep a record of:

- the full range of preparatory tasks which you have been involved with
- changes required to the preparatory tasks as a result of changes to the service requirements
- changes to the preparatory tasks as a result of meeting differing customer needs
- difficulties which you have experienced and how these difficulties have been overcome

Taking bookings

When a customer makes a booking it is often the first point of contact with your establishment. This is an opportunity to give a good first impression of your establishment through assisting with the customer's requests and advising them of the services your establishment provides.

In taking bookings you should be able to:

❖ demonstrate ability in taking bookings from customers in person, over the phone or by letter

❖ demonstrate your knowledge of the services provided by the establishment, for example opening times, menus, beverages and prices

❖ operate within the constraints of the establishment, for instance requiring confirmation, non-overbooking and taking special requests

Learning activities

Read *Food and Beverage Service* Chapter 5.3 and:
● list the essential information required for a booking
● note how to check that the information you have been given is correct

Review Sections 4 and 6 (pages 56–58) of this book and identify:
● any further activities which you need to undertake with regard to the needs of customers
● any further information you may need on the menu, beverages and other services offered by your establishment

For your establishment make notes on:
● the booking routines and procedures
● those times when written confirmation of deposits may need to be taken
● who has the authority to accept or reject bookings
● the procedures for dealing with special requests
● which other areas need to be informed of the booking requirements and how this is carried out

Together with colleagues or your supervisor discuss:
● the range of food and beverages which are available and their prices

- services available from your establishment
- opening times
- booking routines and procedures

Through being observed by your colleagues or your supervisor, while at work, assess:
- your ability to take bookings from customers in person, over the phone or by letter
- your ability to explain the menu, beverages and other service offered by the establishment, and the prices and times of availability
- those areas where you are competent
- those areas where you will need to undertake some additional learning

With your supervisor discuss:
- the extent to which you are meeting the establishment requirements for the taking of bookings
- areas where you feel you are competent
- areas where you both agree some further learning would be valuable.

While you are at work keep a record of:
- the range of methods you have been involved in for taking bookings
- the range of bookings you have taken
- those times when your contribution has helped to ensure a lack of difficulties with bookings
- times when things have gone wrong and how these situations have been resolved

Receiving customers

The welcome is an essential part of the service process. It is a chance for you to help the customer feel at home and within a friendly environment.

In receiving customers you should be able to:

❖ meet, greet and seat customers within the service area

❖ take note and act upon customer requirements

❖ direct and advise customers in a variety of service situations

Learning activities

Read *Food and Beverage Service* Section 5.5 and make notes on:
● the various stages in the service of a meal

For your establishment make notes on:
● the procedures and routines for the greeting and receiving of customers
● the particular routines for informing other areas of the customer arrival
● procedures for dealing with special requests
● procedures for dealing with the special needs of customers

Together with your colleagues or supervisor discuss:
● the procedures and routines required by your establishment in the receiving of customers
● the procedure for dealing with special requests and special needs
● the extent to which you are familiar with the establishment requirements
● areas where you will need to undertake some further learning

Through being observed by your colleagues or your supervisor while at work, assess:
● the extent to which you are receiving guests in the manner required by the establishment
● the extent to which you are responding to special requests or special needs
● those areas where you will need to undertake further learning

With your supervisor review:

- your contribution to customers being received according to the establishment requirements
- those aspects in which you both agree you are performing competently
- those areas where you will need to undertake some further learning

While at work keep a record of:

- your progress in developing your ability in receiving customers
- the range of special requests or special needs you have dealt with
- the range of types and sizes of parties of customers you have received
- difficulties which have arisen and how these have been dealt with

Taking food and beverage orders

The taking and recording of food and beverage orders provides the essential communication link between the service and the customer. Whichever method your establishment has chosen the ultimate goal is still the same – to inform a range of areas within the establishment what the customer has ordered.

In taking food and beverage orders you should be able to:

❖ operate within the establishment requirements for the efficient taking of orders

❖ provide explanations of the items on offer and the service requirements

❖ provide advice on food and wine harmony as requested

❖ take orders from a variety of customers including adults, children, those with mobility difficulties, those with communication difficulties and those with special dietary needs

❖ identify the orders of individual customers in a party

Learning activities

Review Sections 4 and 6 (pages 56–58) of this book and identify:
● additional learning activities which you may need to undertake in order to support you in taking food and beverage orders

Read *Food and Beverage Service* Section 5.6 or *The Beverage Book* Chapter 11 and make notes on:
● the purpose of taking orders
● the different methods of taking orders
● the various stages in the service of a meal where orders may need to be taken
● the variety of customers from whom orders may need to be taken, especially customers with special needs

For your establishment make notes on:
● the procedures and routines for the taking of food and beverage orders
● the procedures for dealing with special requests
● the procedures for dealing with the special needs of customers
● the methods used to ensure that every customer in a party gets the correct order

Together with your colleagues or supervisor discuss:
- the procedures and routines required by your establishment in the taking of food and beverage orders
- the procedure for dealing with special requests and special needs
- the extent to which you are able to explain the menu and beverages on offer
- the extent to which you are able to make appropriate suggestions to customers on choices
- the extent to which you are familiar with the establishment requirements
- areas where you will need to undertake some further learning

Through being observed by your colleagues or your supervisor while at work, assess:
- the extent to which you are taking food and beverage orders according to the procedures and routines of your establishment
- the extent to which you are responding to special requests, or to special needs
- your ability to respond to requests for suggestions on food choices and food and wine harmony
- your ability to identify which member of a party made a particular order
- those areas where you will need to undertake further learning

With your supervisor review:
- your contribution to the efficient taking of food and beverage orders
- those aspects in which you both agree you are performing competently
- those areas where you will need to undertake some further learning

During work times make a record of:
- your progress in developing your ability in taking food and beverage orders
- the range of special requests or special needs you have dealt with
- the type and size of parties of customers you have taken orders from
- the range of advice you have been asked for
- difficulties which have arisen and how these have been dealt with

Serving food

There are good reasons, both practical and traditional, behind the various conventions for the service of food. Good training and practice is the only way of becoming proficient in the service of food. Increasing technical ability, along with experience, will help to raise your confidence while serving.

Serving food proficiently means you should be able to:

❖ demonstrate practical ability in the service of all menu items

❖ observe the establishment conventions in the service of food

❖ use appropriate skills and hygienic and safe working practices at all times

❖ demonstrate a logical and efficient method of working

❖ deal with customer requirements and special requests as they arise

❖ contribute to the team-working requirements of the establishment

❖ adopt appropriate liaison with other staff working within the food and beverage area

Learning activities

Review Sections 4 to 6 of this book and make notes on:
● any additional learning activities you may need to undertake to assist you in the service of food

Read *Food and Beverage Service* Sections 5.5 and 5.7 and make notes on:
● the various points in a meal where the service of food takes place
● the range of food items which require serving
● the various methods for serving food items
● the conventions for service (for example the side of the table)

For your establishment make notes on:
● the full range of menu items
● the service requirements for each menu item
● the accompaniments for each item

Together with your colleagues or supervisor discuss:
● the service requirements for each menu item
● the procedure for dealing with special requests and special needs

- the accompaniment requirements for each menu item
- the extent to which you are familiar with the establishment requirements
- areas where you will need to undertake some further learning

Through being observed during service, either by your colleagues or your supervisor, assess:
- your ability to serve customers' food orders to the establishment's standards
- your service of accompaniments
- the extent to which you work in a hygienic and safe manner
- the extent to which you work in a logical and efficient manner
- your contribution to the work of the team
- your ability to anticipate requirements and deal with requests from customers
- your liaison and help to others when appropriate

With your supervisor review:
- your contribution to the efficient service of food orders
- those aspects in which you both agree you are performing competently
- those areas where you will need to undertake some further learning

During work times keep a record of:
- your progress in developing your ability in the service of food orders
- the range of special meals you have served
- the range of types of parties you have served
- the range of advice you have been asked for when serving food orders
- difficulties which have arisen and how these have been dealt with

Serving beverages

Serving beverages is a task which requires good technical and interpersonal skills, as well as talent and knowledge.

In serving beverages you should be able to:

❖ advise customers on their choice of beverages, including explaining the content and methods of production

❖ demonstrate practical ability in the service of a range of beverages

❖ observe the establishment conventions in the service of beverages

❖ operate within legal requirements governing the sale of alcoholic beverages

❖ use appropriate skills and hygienic and safe working practices at all times

❖ demonstrate a logical and efficient method of working

❖ deal with customer requirements and special requests as they arise

❖ contribute to the team-working requirements of the establishment

❖ adopt appropriate liaison with other staff working within the food and beverage area

Learning activities

Review Sections 4 to 6 of this book and make notes on:
● any additional learning activities you may need to undertake to assist you in the service of alcoholic and non-alcoholic beverages

Read *Food and Beverage Service* Sections 5.5, 5.8 and 10.1 and/or *The Beverage Book* Chapters 1 and 11 and make notes on:
● the legal requirements for the sale of alcoholic liquor
● the various points in meal service where beverages may be served
● the various alcoholic and non-alcoholic beverages which require serving
● the various methods for serving beverage orders
● the conventions for service (for example the side of the table)

For your establishment make notes on
● the type of licensing provision for the sale of alcoholic *liquor*
● the full range of alcoholic and non-alcoholic beverages on offer
● the service requirements for every beverage on offer

Together with your colleagues or supervisor discuss:
- the licensing law requirements for the sale of alcoholic *liquor*
- the service requirements for all alcoholic and non-alcoholic beverages on offer
- the procedure for dealing with special requests and special needs
- recommendations for beverages to accompany any of the food items on offer
- the extent to which you are familiar with the establishment requirements
- areas where you will need to undertake some further learning

Through being observed during service, either by your colleagues or your supervisor, assess:
- your ability to serve alcoholic and non-alcoholic beverages to the establishment standards
- the extent to which you work in a hygienic and safe manner
- the extent to which you work in a logical and efficient manner
- your contribution to the work of the team
- your ability to anticipate requirements and deal with requests from customers
- your liaison and help to others when appropriate

With your supervisor review:
- your contribution to efficient beverage service
- those aspects in which you both agree you are performing competently
- those areas where you will need to undertake some further learning

During work times keep a record of:
- your progress in developing your ability in beverage service
- the range of beverages you have served
- the range of types of parties you have served
- the range of advice you have been asked for when serving beverages
- difficulties which have arisen and how these have been dealt with

Clearing

Efficient clearing during service will speed service, avoid the customer having to remain with used items, and give an impression of professional ability. Clearing in a professional manner will also help to increase efficiency and minimise breakages through incorrect handling.

In carrying out clearing during service you should be able to:

❖ demonstrate ability in the clearing of customer tables

❖ demonstrate ability in the clearing of food and beverage service areas

❖ undertake clearing with regard to the convenience of customers

❖ adopt safe and hygienic working practices

❖ demonstrate logical and efficient work methods

❖ contribute to the team-working requirements of the establishment

❖ adopt appropriate liaison with other staff working within the food and beverage area

Learning activities

Review Sections 5 and 6 of this book and make notes on:
● any additional learning activities you should undertake to support you in developing your ability in clearing.

Read *Food and Beverage Service* Sections 5.5 and 5.10 on clearing and make notes on:
● the various points in meal service where clearing may need to take place
● the various items which require clearing
● the various methods of clearing

For your establishment make notes on:
● the range of items which need clearing
● the clearing methods for all items

Together with your colleagues or supervisor discuss:
● the items which require clearing during service
● the methods used for clearing
● the extent to which you are familiar with the establishment requirements
● areas where you will need to undertake some further learning

Through being observed during service, either by your colleagues or your supervisor, assess:

- your ability to clear the full variety of items required in your establishment
- the extent to which you work in a hygienic and safe manner
- the extent to which you work in a logical and efficient manner
- your contribution to the work of the team
- your ability to anticipate requirements and deal with requests from customers
- your liaison and help to others when appropriate

With your supervisor review:

- your contribution to efficient clearing
- those aspects in which you both agree you are performing competently
- those areas where you will need to undertake some further learning

During work times keep a record of:

- your progress in developing your clearing ability
- the range of items you have cleared
- the range of types of parties you have cleared for
- difficulties which have arisen and how these have been dealt with

Billing and cashiering

Billing and the control of revenue is a very responsible job, which requires concentration and the ability to be security minded. A pleasant meal can be spoilt for the customer through mistakes with bills, and may even raise question of honesty even if a mistake was genuine.

In order to carry out billing and cashiering duties you should be able to:

- ❖ carry out the establishment's procedures for billing customers
- ❖ observe the requirements for security and credit allowances
- ❖ undertake cashiering duties according to the establishment requirements
- ❖ handle a variety of payment methods – cash and cash equivalent
- ❖ exchange foreign cash and travellers' cheques
- ❖ complete point of sale control requirements including the preparation of summary sheets and other reports

Learning activities

Read *Food and Beverage Service* Sections 5.11 and 10.2 on billing methods and revenue control and make notes on:
- ● the various methods of billing
- ● the various payment methods
- ● the requirements for revenue control

For your establishment make notes on:
- ● how checks are posted onto the customer bill
- ● the billing method used
- ● the payment methods accepted
- ● security checks for the various payment methods
- ● the procedures for operating payment points
- ● the revenue control procedures in operation
- ● security arrangements for cash and equivalents

Together with your colleagues or supervisor discuss:
- ● the establishment procedures for billing customers
- ● security requirements and credit allowances
- ● the routines for cashiering duties
- ● the variety of acceptable payment methods – cash and cash equivalent

- the routines and restrictions on exchanging foreign cash and travellers' cheques
- the point of sale control requirements including the preparation of summary sheets and other reports

Through being observed when undertaking billing and/or cashiering duties, either by your colleagues or your supervisor, assess:
- your ability to complete bills according to the establishment requirements
- your handling of a variety of payments
- your dealing with foreign cash or travellers' cheques
- the completion of sales summaries
- the extent to which you work in a logical and efficient manner
- your contribution to the work of the team
- your liaison and help to others when appropriate

With your supervisor review:
- your contribution to efficient billing and cashiering
- those aspects in which you both agree you are performing competently
- those areas where you will need to undertake some further learning

During work times keep a record of:
- your progress in developing your ability in billing and cashiering
- the range of payment methods you have dealt with
- handling appropriate security routines
- difficulties which have arisen and how these have been dealt with

Clearing following service

Clearing at the end of service must be carried out both for security and hygiene reasons, as well as assisting the smooth running of the establishment.

In performing clearing duties you should be able to:

❖ clear areas according to the routines of the establishment

❖ adopt safe and hygienic working practices

❖ ensure the security requirements of the establishment are maintained

❖ ensure appropriate action for the storage of food items

❖ contribute to the team-working requirements of the establishment

❖ adopt appropriate liaison with other staff working within the food and beverage area

Learning activities

Review Sections 5 and 6 of this book and make notes on:
- any additional learning you will need to undertake in order for you to contribute to the clearing of the areas after service

Read *Food and Beverage Service* Section 5.12 and:
- list the various clearing duties that may need to be undertaken in the food service areas

For your establishment make notes on:
- the full range of clearing duties that are required
- your specific responsibilities in undertaking these activities
- the procedures and systems to be observed when undertaking clearing tasks
- how these tasks are being assessed to ensure that they meet the requirements of the establishment
- how stock levels of items such as cutlery, glassware, paper, linen and so on are determined
- the procedure for ordering replacement stock

Together with your colleagues or your supervisor check your knowledge of the clearing tasks and make notes on:
- the extent to which you know of all the clearing tasks required

- the extent to which you are able to describe your contribution to the clearing requirements
- areas where you are confident in your knowledge of the requirements
- areas where you will need to undertake further work

Through being observed while at work, either by your colleagues or supervisor, make notes on:

- your ability to carry out the clearing tasks expected of you
- the meeting of health and safety requirements
- the extent to which you are working in a logical and efficient manner
- those areas where you are meeting the requirements of the establishment
- those areas where you still have additional learning or practice to undertake

Together with a colleague or your supervisor carry out an after-service check for your service area and make notes on:

- those areas where you have met the establishment requirements
- those areas where you have not met the requirements
- aspects of the clearing which have been affected by things outside your control
- how you intend to follow these aspects up
- areas where you will need to undertake further practice or training

Arrange to review your contribution to preparatory tasks with your supervisor in order to:

- establish those areas where you are both happy about your contribution
- those areas where you are fully working within the requirements of the establishment
- those areas where you would like more guidance
- those areas where you will need to undertake further work

During work times keep a record of:

- the full range of clearing tasks you have been involved with
- changes required to the clearing tasks as a result of changes to the service requirements
- difficulties which you have experienced and how these difficulties have been overcome

DEVELOPING SPECIALISED SERVICE SKILLS

Breakfasts

Breakfast, be it a continental or full breakfast, is one of the most important meals of the day. The service of breakfasts may be your main role or a part of your role in food and beverage service. Each establishment will have their own procedures.

For breakfast service you should be able to:

❖ appreciate customer needs for breakfast service

❖ operate within health, safety and security requirements

❖ demonstrate your familiarity with the service areas associated with breakfast service

❖ use equipment for breakfast service

❖ demonstrate your knowledge of the menu, beverage items and other services offered at breakfast time

❖ demonstrate the service skills necessary in order to serve breakfasts well

Learning activities

You should collect information and make notes on:
● the service requirement of breakfasts within your establishment

Read *Food and Beverage Service* Section 6.1 and note:
● the similarities and differences between the published information and the requirements of your establishment

Ask your supervisor to discuss with you your current abilities in food and beverage service and record:
● areas where you and your supervisor believe you are already competent
● areas where you and your supervisor believe you are not competent
● areas where it will be necessary for you to undertake further learning in order for you to be competent in the service of breakfasts

Read Sections 4 to 7 of this book in order to identify learning activities which you could undertake to enhance your performance and list:
● the learning activities you are intending to undertake

Through being observed by your colleagues or supervisor test your knowledge of the requirements for breakfast service and record:
- areas where you are competent
- areas where you still have some work to do

 Through being observed by your colleagues and supervisor test your skill, interpersonal and technical, in the service of breakfasts and record:
- areas where you are competent
- areas where you still have some work to do

 During work times keep a record of:
- the range of food and beverages you are serving
- the range of customers you are serving
- the range of differing requests which you have been asked for and how you have dealt with these

Afternoon teas

Afternoon tea, in all its various forms, remains a popular meal and serving this is often a part of the server's role alongside service at other times. Each establishment will have its own procedures.

For afternoon teas you should be able to:

❖ appreciate customer needs for afternoon tea

❖ operate within health, safety and security requirements

❖ demonstrate your familiarity with the service areas associated with the service of afternoon tea

❖ use equipment for the service of afternoon tea

❖ demonstrate knowledge of the menu, beverage items and other services offered for afternoon tea

❖ demonstrate the service skills necessary in order to serve afternoon teas well

Learning activities

You should collect information and make notes on:
● the service requirements of afternoon teas within your establishment.

Read *Food and Beverage Service* Section 6.2 and note:
● the similarities and differences between the published information and the requirements of your establishment

Ask your supervisor to discuss with you your current abilities in food and beverage service and record:
● areas where you and your supervisor believe you are already competent
● areas where you and your supervisor believe you are not competent
● additional areas where you will need to undertake further learning in order to be competent in the service of afternoon teas

Read Sections 4 to 7 of this book in order to identify learning activities which you could undertake to enhance your performance and list:
● the learning activities you are intending to undertake

Through being observed by your colleagues or supervisor test your knowledge of the requirements for the service of afternoon teas and record:
- areas where you are competent
- areas where you still have some work to do

 Through being observed by your colleagues or supervisor test your skill, interpersonal and technical, in the service of afternoon teas and record:
- areas where you are competent
- areas where you still have some work to do

 When you are at work keep a record of:
- the range of food and beverages you are serving
- the range of customers you are serving
- the range of differing requests which you have been asked for and how you have dealt with these

Room service

Room or floor service in hotels can cover a wide range of food and beverage items within a range of meals. Room or floor service may be your main role or a part of your role in food and beverage service. Each establishment will have its own procedures.

For room service you should be able to:

❖ appreciate customer needs for room service

❖ operate within health, safety and security requirements

❖ demonstrate your familiarity with the service areas associated with room service

❖ use equipment for the provision of room service

❖ demonstrate knowledge of the menu, beverage items and other services offered by your establishment for room service

❖ demonstrate the service skills necessary in order to perform room service well

Learning activities

You should collect information and make notes on:
- the service requirements of room service within your establishment

Read *Food and Beverage Service* Section 7.2 and note:
- the similarities and differences between the published information and the requirements of your establishment

Ask your supervisor to discuss with you your current abilities in food and beverage service and record:
- areas where you and your supervisor believe you are already competent
- areas where you and your supervisor believe you are not competent
- additional areas where you will need to undertake further learning in order to be competent in room service

Read Sections 4 to 7 of this book in order to identify learning activities which you could undertake to enhance your performance and list:
- the learning activities you are intending to undertake

Through being observed by your colleagues or supervisor test your knowledge of the requirements for room service in your establishment and record:
● areas where you are competent
● areas where you still have some work to do

Through being observed by your colleagues or supervisor test your skill, interpersonal and technical, in carrying out room service and record:
● areas where you are competent
● areas where you still have some work to do

When you are at work keep a record of:
● the range of food and beverages you are serving
● the range of customers you are serving
● the range of differing requests which you have been asked for and how you have dealt with these

Lounge service

Lounge service is offered in a variety of hotels and other types of establishment. There are also a wide variety of service settings, food and beverage items within a range of meals. Lounge service may be your main role or it may be part of your role in food and beverage service. Each establishment will have its own procedures.

For lounge service you should be able to:

❖ appreciate customer needs for lounge service
❖ operate within health, safety and security requirements
❖ demonstrate your familiarity with the service areas associated with the provision of lounge service
❖ use equipment for lounge service
❖ demonstrate your knowledge of the menu, beverage items and other services offered for lounge service
❖ demonstrate the service skills necessary in order to perform lounge service well

Learning activities

You should collect information and make notes on:
● the service requirements for lounge service within your establishment

Read *Food and Beverage Service* Section 7.3 and note:
● the similarities and differences between the published information and the requirements of your establishment

Ask your supervisor to discuss with you your current abilities in food and beverage service and record:
● areas where you and your supervisor believe you are already competent
● areas where you and your supervisor believe you are not competent
● additional areas where you will need to undertake further learning in order to be competent in lounge service

Read Sections 4 to 7 of this book in order to identify learning activities which you could undertake to enhance your performance and list:
● the learning activities you are intending to undertake

Through being observed by your colleagues or supervisor test your knowledge of the requirements for lounge service in your establishment and record:
- areas where you are competent
- areas where you still have some work to do

Through being observed by your colleagues or supervisor test your skill, interpersonal and technical, in lounge service in your establishment and record:
- areas where you are competent
- areas where you still have some work to do

When you are at work keep a record of:
- the range of food and beverages you are serving
- the range of customers you are serving
- the range of differing requests which you have been asked for and how you have dealt with these

Guéridon service

Guéridon service is an extension of food and beverage service which will require you to develop an additional range of service skills. Guéridon service in its most simple form is where the guéridon is used as a side-table, from where food items are transferred onto the customer's plate before the plate is placed in front of the customer. In a more advanced form the use of the guéridon may provide for the carving, filleting or jointing of items in the food service area and also the preparation and cooking of dishes.

For guéridon service you should be able to:

❖ appreciate customer needs for guéridon service
❖ operate within health, safety and security requirements
❖ demonstrate your familiarity with the service areas associated with guéridon service
❖ use the equipment for guéridon service
❖ demonstrate your knowledge of the menu, ingredients and beverage items used in guéridon service
❖ demonstrate service skills necessary in order to undertake guéridon service well

Depending on the establishment you should also be able to:

❖ carve, fillet, joint and serve dishes at the table
❖ prepare and serve food using a guéridon
❖ cook and finish dishes in a food service area

Learning activities

You should collect information and make notes on:
● the service requirements for guéridon service within your establishment

Read *Food and Beverage Service* Chapter 8 and note:
● the similarities and differences between the published information and the requirements of your establishment

Ask your supervisor to discuss with you your current abilities in food and beverage service and record:
● areas where you and your supervisor believe you are already competent

- areas where you and your supervisor believe you are not competent
- additional areas where you will need to undertake further learning in order to be competent in guéridon service

Read Sections 4 to 7 of this book in order to identify learning activities which you could undertake to enhance your performance and list:
- the learning activities you are intending to undertake

For your own establishment you should collect information and make notes on:
- recipes, methods and procedures for dishes which are served using the guéridon
- any limitations on the number and range of dishes which can be served at any one time

Through being observed by your colleagues or supervisor test your knowledge of the requirements for guéridon service in your establishment and record:
- areas where you are competent
- areas where you still have some work to do

Through being observed by your colleagues or supervisor test your skill, interpersonal and technical, in guéridon service in your establishment and record:
- areas where you are competent
- areas where you still have some work to do

Ask your supervisor to discuss with you:
- alternative methods and procedures for the dishes currently on offer
- alternative dishes which may be appropriate for guéridon service

When you are at work keep a record of:
- the range of guéridon service activities you are undertaking
- the range of customers you are serving
- the range of differing requests which you have been asked for and how you have dealt with these
- any difficult situations you have been faced with and how you have handled these

WORKING IN FUNCTION CATERING

Preparing for and serving at functions

Function or event catering, or banqueting, is a very varied aspect of food and beverage service. You may be working in this type of food and beverage service as your main role, or as part of your role. Each establishment will have its own procedures.

For function catering you should be able to:

❖ appreciate customer needs in function catering

❖ operate within health, safety and security requirements

❖ demonstrate knowledge of the service areas associated with function catering

❖ use equipment for function catering

❖ demonstrate knowledge of the menu, beverage items and other services offered as part of function catering

❖ demonstrate the service skills necessary in order to serve well at functions

Learning activities

You should collect information and make notes on:
● the service requirements of functions within your establishment

Read *Food and Beverage Service* Section 9.1 and note:
● the similarities and differences between the published information and the requirements of your establishment

Ask your supervisor to discuss with you your current abilities in food and beverage service and record:
● areas where you and your supervisor believe you are already competent
● areas where you and your supervisor believe you are not competent
● areas where it will be necessary for you to undertake further learning in order for you to be competent in serving at functions

Read Sections 4 to 7 of this book in order to identify learning activities which you could undertake to enhance your performance and list:
● the learning activities you are intending to undertake

Through being observed by your colleagues or supervisor test your knowledge of the requirements for functions at your establishment and record:
- areas where you are competent
- areas where you still have some work to do

Through being observed test your skill, interpersonal and technical, in service at functions at your establishment and record:
- areas where you are competent
- areas where you still have some work to do

During work times keep a record of:
- the range of food and beverages you are serving
- the range of customers you are serving
- the range of differing requests which you have been asked for and how you have dealt with these

Contribute to function administration

Function administration is concerned with the providing of sales information, handling bookings and supporting the information flow necessary for the various departments involved. It also involves working together for the success of the function, event, banquet or conference.

In contributing to function administration you should be able to:

❖ appreciate customer needs in function catering

❖ operate within health, safety and security requirements

❖ demonstrate your knowledge of the menu and beverages on offer together with the range of services offered by your establishment

❖ demonstrate your knowledge of the procedures necessary for the administration of functions in your establishment

❖ advise customers on the menu, beverages and other services

❖ take bookings for functions according to the establishment procedures

❖ follow the administrative requirements for ensuring the booking is recorded correctly

❖ follow the administrative requirements for informing other departments of the bookings

❖ anticipate likely problem areas and take appropriate action

Learning activities

You should collect information and make notes on:

● the administration requirements of functions, events, banquets, special parties and conferences within your establishment

Read *Food and Beverage Service* Sections 9.1 and 9.2 and note:

● the similarities and differences between the published information and the requirements of your establishment

Read Sections 4 to 7 of this book in order to identify learning activities which you could undertake to enhance your performance and list:

● the learning activities you are intending to undertake

Through being observed by your colleagues or supervisor test your knowledge of the requirements for function administration at your establishment and record:

- areas where you are competent
- areas where you still have some work to do

Through being observed by your colleagues or supervisor test your skill, interpersonal and technical, in the administration of functions at your establishment and record:

- areas where you are competent
- areas where you still have some work to do

Ask your supervisor to review with you your current abilities in function administration and record:

- areas where you and your supervisor believe you are already competent
- areas where you and your supervisor believe you are not competent
- additional areas where you will need to undertake further learning in order to be competent in the serving at functions

During work times keep a record of:

- the range of types of function you are booking and carrying out the administration for
- the range of customers making the bookings
- the range of differing requests which you have been asked for and how you have dealt with these

Contribute to function organisation

Function organisation is concerned with translating the booking requirements into a well-run function, event, banquet or conference.

In contributing to the organisation of a function you should be able to:

- ❖ appreciate customer needs in function catering
- ❖ operate within health, safety and security requirements
- ❖ demonstrate your knowledge of the menu, beverages and service available in your establishment for functions
- ❖ demonstrate your knowledge of the capabilities of the staff, equipment and facilities of your establishment
- ❖ communicate to other departments involved to ensure the smooth running of the function
- ❖ allocate tasks to various staff as required for the function
- ❖ anticipate potential problem areas and take appropriate action

Learning activities

You should collect information and make notes on:
- the service requirements of function organisation within your establishment

Read *Food and Beverage Service* Sections 9.3 and 9.4 and note:
- the similarities and differences between the published information and the requirements of your establishment

Read Sections 4 to 8 of this book in order to identify learning activities which you could undertake to enhance your performance and list:
- the learning activities you are intending to undertake

Through being observed by your colleagues or supervisor test your knowledge of the requirements for function organisation at your establishment and record:
- areas where you are competent
- areas where you still have some work to do

Through being observed by your colleagues or supervisor test your skill, interpersonal and technical, in function organisation at your establishment and record:
● areas where you are competent
● areas where you still have some work to do

During working keep a record of:
● the range of types of function you are organising
● the range of customers the functions are for
● the range of differing requests which you have been asked for and how you have dealt with these

Ask your supervisor to discuss with you your current abilities in function organisation and record:
● areas where you and your supervisor believe you are already competent
● areas where you and your supervisor believe you are not competent
● areas where it will be necessary for you to undertake further learning in order for you to be competent in serving at functions

DEVELOPING SUPERVISORY ABILITIES

Supervise food and beverage operations within licensing (and other) laws

Food and beverage operations are governed by a range of legislation which must be complied with. These laws range from the control of the sale of alcoholic liquor to health and safety requirements. There are also laws, for instance, which cover the relationship between the customer and the business.

In supervising food and beverage operations within licensing and other laws you should be able to:

- ❖ identify the relevant legislation applicable to the provision of food and beverage service
- ❖ determine the requirements which will need to be met in order to comply with the legislation
- ❖ ensure that staff and customers are informed of the implications of legislation
- ❖ ensure routines are in place to deal with breaches, both for customers and staff, of legal requirements

Learning activities

Read *Food and Beverage Service* Section 10.1 and make notes on:
- types of licences available and what each type of licence allows
- how the licensing legislation affects the sale of alcohol to young persons
- requirements of weights and measures for the sale of intoxicating liquor
- how contract law affects your establishment
- requirements for the sale of goods and trades descriptions
- potential discrimination
- obligations to provide services
- requirements for price lists
- service, cover and minimum charges
- responsibilities for customer property and rights regarding customer debt
- health, safety and security requirements
- other legislative requirements not covered in Section 10.1

For your establishment make notes on:
- the type of licence(s) your establishment holds
- what other laws need to be observed within your establishment
- where you can obtain copies of these laws
- the procedures in your establishment for ensuring compliance with legislative controls
- your limit of authority
- those with the powers of entry and enforcement

Together with your colleagues or supervisor assess your knowledge of:
- legislation which affects your establishment
- the interpretation of the requirements
- routines for ensuring compliance amongst staff and customers
- procedures which are undertaken where breaches take place
- your limit of authority
- areas where you need to undertake some further investigation

Through being observed by your colleagues or supervisor assess the extent to which you:
- are able to answer questions from staff and customers on legislative requirements
- handle breaches of regulations by staff or customers with care
- take appropriate action on ensuring the legislation is complied with
- undertake appropriate briefing and training of staff

Discuss your progress and record your:
- strengths and weaknesses in ensuring compliance with legislation
- ability to communicate the requirements to customers and staff
- areas where you both agree that your performance is competent
- areas where you need to undertake some further work

During work times keep a record of:
- initiatives which you have implemented to ensure compliance with the legal requirements
- situations where you have had to deal with breaches of the legislation by customers and staff
- difficulties which you have faced and how these were overcome

Contributing to the control of food and beverage operations

The control of food and beverage operations is part of a supervisor's responsibilities. Control is concerned with the management and security of stock, the control of revenue and the recording of the information required so informed decisions can be made about the performance of the operation.

In contributing to the control of food and beverage operations you should be able to:

❖ ensure that routines for the ordering, receiving, storage and control of beverages and other stocks are adequately adhered to

❖ identify and check on the required environmental storage conditions

❖ ensure that appropriate handling and stock rotation is applied

❖ maintain the payment points and the handling of cash and cash equivalents

❖ check to ensure that accurate records are maintained

❖ identify and take action where legislation is not being complied with

❖ produce and interpret a variety of management reports

❖ deal with unforeseen situations

Learning activities

Read *Food and Beverage Service* Sections 10.2, 10.3 and 10.4 or *The Beverage Book* Chapter 8 and make notes on:

● factors to be considered in the supervision of food and beverage control

● the various stages of the ordering, purchasing, storing and issuing process

● methods of control of stock and revenue

● the calculation of usage and profit

● the calculation of a variety of performance measures

For your establishment make notes on:

● routines for ordering, receiving, storing and issuing stock

● environmental conditions for storage which need to be maintained

● limits of authority for those involved

● how security of the stock is maintained

- how the security of revenue is maintained
- how stock-taking is carried out
- how new staff are trained
- recording and reporting requirements on the food and beverage operation

With your colleagues or your supervisor assess your knowledge of:
- establishment policies for the ordering, receiving, storage and issuing of stock
- administration requirements for stock control
- legislative requirements which need to be complied with
- limits of authority of various members of staff
- needs for security in food and beverage operations
- the recording and reporting requirements
- how to calculate and interpret performance measures
- areas where you may need to undertake some further investigation

Through being observed while at work assess the extent to which you:
- are able to answer questions from staff and customers on control requirements
- handle non-compliance with establishment requirements by staff
- take appropriate action on ensuring the maintenance of security
- undertake appropriate briefing and training of staff

Together with your supervisor discuss:
- the extent to which you are meeting the establishment requirements for the supervision of the food and beverage operation
- your identification of aspects which require attention in the training of staff or in alterations to procedures
- areas where you will need to undertake further investigation or training

During work times keep records of:
- the training you have received
- initiatives which you have implemented to ensure improved security or efficiency of the food and beverage operation
- situations where you have had to handle non-compliance with establishment requirements by staff
- difficulties which you have faced and how these were overcome

Maintaining the cleaning programme in your own area

One of the five key factors which affect the customer's enjoyment of the meal experience is the cleanliness and hygiene of an establishment (see *Food and Beverage Service* Section 1.5). In addition there are health and safety regulations which must be complied with.

In maintaining the cleaning programme in your area you should be able to:

❖ demonstrate that the establishment procedures are effectively communicated to staff

❖ ensure the stock of cleaning materials is maintained

❖ carry out inspections to ensure that the establishment routines are being maintained

❖ ensure that appropriate action is taken to ensure the maintenance of the cleaning programme

❖ ensure that the required records are maintained

❖ ensure that feedback on the effectiveness of the cleaning programme is obtained and appropriate action taken

❖ present proposals for required changes to the cleaning routines

❖ determine the extent to which the cleaning routines are in line with relevant legislation

Learning activities

Read *Food and Beverage Service* Section 10.6 on cleaning routines and make notes on:
● factors to be considered in the development and maintenance of cleaning routines

For your establishment make notes on:
● establishment procedures for cleaning schedules
● systems for the maintenance of materials for cleaning
● requirements for you to carry out inspections
● responsibilities to ensure that the establishment routines are being maintained
● action to be taken to ensure the maintenance of the cleaning programme
● the required records

- feedback requirements on the effectiveness of the cleaning programme
- routines for proposing required changes to the cleaning routines
- the legislation which the cleaning routines needs to comply with

With your colleagues or with your supervisor assess your knowledge of:
- establishment requirements for cleaning routines
- administration requirements for stock control
- legislative requirements which need to be complied with
- limits of authority of various members of staff
- needs for cleaning in food and beverage operations
- recording and reporting requirements
- how action can be taken on feedback which has been obtained
- areas where you may need to undertake some further investigation

Through being observed while at work assess the extent to which you:
- are able to answer questions from staff and customers on cleaning routines
- handle non-compliance with establishment requirements by staff
- take appropriate action on ensuring the maintenance of the cleaning programme
- undertake appropriate briefing and training of staff

Together with your supervisor discuss:
- the extent to which you are meeting the establishment requirements for maintenance of the cleaning programme
- your identification of aspects which require attention in the training of staff or in alterations to procedures
- areas where you will need to undertake further investigation or training

During work times keep records of:
- the training you have received
- initiatives which you have implemented to ensure improvements in the effectiveness of the cleaning programme
- situations where you have had to handle non-compliance with establishment requirements by staff
- difficulties which you have faced and how these were overcome

Maintaining the vending machine services

Vending machines are often used to augment food and beverage operations. While they are valuable to support operations, there are considerable requirements in the cleaning and maintenance of the systems to support this service.

In maintaining the vending machine service you should be able to:

❖ demonstrate that the service meets client needs

❖ develop routines which ensure the efficiency of the operation

❖ ensure that relevant legislation is complied with

❖ provide regular briefings to staff on changes to the product or the customer demand

❖ seek and take action on feedback from staff on the service operation

❖ ensure records are maintained and required reports completed

❖ carry out sales analysis and determine informed recommendations

❖ ensure payment systems are maintained

❖ carry out inspections on all aspects of the operation and take action on the outcome

Learning activities

Read *Food and Beverage Service* Sections 2.8 and 2.15 and make notes on:
- the range of services offered through vending
- factors to be considered in the provision of a vending service

For your establishment make notes on:
- client needs which the vending service is intended to meet
- establishment routines which ensure the efficiency of the operation
- relevant legislation which the service will need to comply with
- needs for regular briefings to staff on changes to the product or customer demand
- methods of obtaining feedback from staff on the service operation
- records and reports required
- methods for sales analysis and the routines for making recommendations

- payment/control systems in use
- requirements for inspections

With your colleagues or with your supervisor assess your knowledge of:
- establishment policies for the provision of the vending service
- administration requirements for the vending service
- legislative requirements which need to be complied with
- limits of authority of various members of staff
- recording and reporting requirements
- making recommendations on changes required as a result of customer or staff feedback
- areas where you may need to undertake some further investigation

Through being observed while at work assess the extent to which you:
- are able to answer questions from staff and customers on the vending service
- handle non-compliance of establishment requirements by staff
- take appropriate action on ensuring the maintenance of the vending service
- undertake appropriate briefing and training of staff

Together with your supervisor discuss:
- the extent to which you are meeting the establishment requirements for the maintenance of the vending service
- your identification of aspects which require attention in the training of staff or in alterations to procedures
- areas where you will need to undertake further investigation or training

During work times keep records of:
- the training you have received
- initiatives which you have implemented to ensure improvements in the vending service
- situations where you have had to handle non-compliance of establishment requirements by staff
- difficulties which you have faced and how these were overcome

Improving service reliability for customers

One of the factors which contribute to maintaining customer satisfaction is the maintenance of high standards of operation.

In improving the service reliability for customers you should be able to:

- ❖ identify and respond to customer service needs
- ❖ demonstrate how customer feedback is sought and acted upon
- ❖ show how initiatives are being taken to improve customer service reliability
- ❖ demonstrate how feedback from staff is acted upon
- ❖ review and take appropriate action on current procedures
- ❖ contribute to and assist in the development of teamwork within the establishment

Learning activities

Read *Food and Beverage Service* Chapter 1 and Section 10.5 and make notes on:
- factors to be considered in meeting customer needs
- critical points in the service and in customer relations

For your establishment make notes on:
- how your establishment identifies and responds to customer service needs
- how customer feedback is sought and acted upon
- what initiatives have been taken to improve customer service reliability
- how feedback from staff has been acted upon
- a review of and possible action to be taken on current procedures
- how you can contribute to and assist in the development of teamwork within the establishment

With your colleagues or with your supervisor assess your knowledge of:
- establishment policies improving the service reliability for customers

- administration requirements
- limits of authority of various members of staff
- needs for improvements in customer service reliability
- recording and reporting requirements
- action which can be taken as a result of feedback from customers or staff
- areas where you may need to undertake some further investigation

Through being observed while at work assess the extent to which you:
- are able to answer questions from staff and customers on improving the service reliability for customers
- are able to identify factors which are contributing to improving service reliability
- take appropriate action on improving service reliability
- undertake appropriate briefing and training of staff

Together with your supervisor discuss:
- the extent to which you are meeting the establishment requirements for improvements in service reliability for customers
- your identification of aspects which require attention in the training of staff or in alterations to current procedures
- areas where you will need to undertake further investigation or training

During work times keep records of:
- the training you have received
- initiatives you have implemented to ensure improved service reliability
- situations where you have responded to feedback from customers or staff
- difficulties which you have faced and how these were overcome

Contributing to the development of teams and individuals

In food and beverage service the staff are the key to a successful operation. As well as individual interpersonal and technical skills, product knowledge and the effectiveness of the team working together are crucial to the smooth running of the establishment.

Contributing to the development needs of individuals and teams means that you should be able to:

❖ identify a range of individual and team needs necessary for the smooth running of the existing operations

❖ have routines which encourage individuals and teams to contribute to the identification of their own development needs

❖ ensure that development needs are related to the aims and objectives of the establishment

❖ make contributions to the planning and implementation of development activities which are relevant to the individuals, the team and the organisation

❖ evaluate the development activities undertaken and report on effectiveness

Learning activities

Read *Food and Beverage Service* Section 10.6 and make notes on:
- the various stages in undertaking training
- the various types of training required
- factors to be considered in developing approaches to training

For your establishment make notes on:
- the range of individual and team needs likely to be necessary for the smooth running of the existing operation
- current routines which encourage individuals and teams to contribute to the identification of their own development needs
- aims and objectives of the establishment in relation to development needs
- your and others' responsibilities for the planning and implementation of development activities
- procedures for the evaluation of the development activities which have been undertaken

With your colleagues or with your supervisor assess your knowledge of:
- establishment policies for meeting the development needs of individuals and teams
- administration requirements
- legislative requirements which may need to be complied with
- limits of authority of various members of staff
- needs for training and development in food and beverage operations
- recording and reporting requirements
- how to identify training and development needs
- areas where you may need to undertake some further investigation

Through being observed while at work assess the extent to which you:
- are able to answer questions from staff on training and development opportunities
- take appropriate action on ensuring that the needs of individuals and teams are identified and met
- undertake appropriate briefing and training of staff

Together with your supervisor discuss:
- the extent to which you are meeting the establishment requirements for development of individuals and teams
- your view of the current effectiveness of the training and development activities being undertaken
- areas where you will need to undertake further investigation or training

During work times keep records of:
- the training you have received
- initiatives you have implemented to ensure improved development of individuals and teams
- difficulties which you have faced and how these were overcome

Implementing sales development activities

Without sales there is no business. Sales development activities are intended to focus on making the most of sales opportunities for the food and beverage operation.

In implementing sales development activities you should be able to:

❖ identify opportunities for sales development activities
❖ make realistic and achievable proposals for sales development activities
❖ plan, implement and review sales development activities

Learning activities

Read *Food and Beverage Service* Chapter 1 and Section 10.7 and make notes on:
- the range of customer needs your establishment is targeted to meet
- factors to be considered in identifying sales opportunities
- various methods which can be used

For your establishment make notes on:
- the range of customer needs your establishment is meeting
- the possibilities that may exist within your current range of customers for additional sales activities
- possibilities which may exist for attracting additional customers to your establishment
- limitations on resources available to you
- your limits of authority
- establishment requirements for the planning, implementation and review of sales development activities

With your colleagues or with your supervisor assess your knowledge of:
- establishment policies for the implementation of sales development activities
- administration requirements for sales development activities
- legislative requirements which need to be complied with
- limits of your authority and that of various members of staff
- needs for the continued sales development activities
- methods of determining resource requirements

- methods for measuring the effectiveness of the activities
- areas where you may need to undertake some further investigation

Through being observed while at work assess the extent to which you:

- make realistic and achievable proposals on sales development activities
- are able to answer questions from staff and customers on sales development activities
- undertake appropriate briefing and training of staff

Together with your supervisor discuss:

- the extent to which you are meeting the establishment requirements for sales development activities
- your identification of aspects which require additional attention in order to improve the effectiveness of the sales development activities
- areas where you will need to undertake further investigation or training

During work times keep records of:

- the training you have received
- examples of presentations you have made
- examples of activities you have undertaken
- initiatives you have implemented to ensure improved effectiveness of sales development activities
- difficulties you have faced and how these were overcome

FURTHER INFORMATION

Learning About Food and Beverage Service is designed to be used in conjunction with two books. These are: *Food and Beverage Service*, written by Dennis Lillicrap, John Cousins and Robert Smith (published by Hodder and Stoughton, 1998) and *The Beverage Book*, written by Andrew Durkan and John Cousins (published by Hodder and Stoughton, 1995).

Further information may be obtained from the following:

Selected published sources

Publication	Author	Published by	Date
Croner's Catering	Edited by Michael Boella	Croner Publications, Ltd	Reference manual with updating service
Caterer and Hotelkeeper	Trade magazine	Reed Business Publications	Weekly
Essential Law for Caterers	Roger Peters	Hodder and Stoughton	1997
Food and Beverage Management	John Cousins, David Foskett and David Shortt	Hodder and Stoughton	1995
Hospitality Accounting	Richard Kotas and Michael Conlan	International Thompson Business Press	1997
Hotel and Food Service Marketing	Francis Buttle	Cassell	1997
Hotel and Restaurant	Trade magazine	Quantum Publishing	Monthly
Human Resource Practice in the Hospitality Industry	John Roberts	Hodder and Stoughton	1997

Larousse Encyclopaedia of Wine	General Editor: Christopher Foulkes	Grantham Book Services	1997
Larousse Gastronomique		Exel Logistics Mandarin	1996
Le Repertoire de la Cuisine	Original French Edition Edouard Brunet. English Edition Louis Saulnier	Leon Jaeggi	1994
Purchasing and Costing for the Hospitality Industry	Denise Drummond	Hodder and Stoughton	1998
Safety in Catering	Roy Hayter	Macmillan	1994
Theory of Catering	Ronald Kinton, Victor Ceserani and David Foskett	Hodder and Stoughton	1995
The Management of Food Service Operations	Peter Jones and Paul Merricks	Cassell	1994

Trade and professional bodies

Académie Culinaire de France (UK)
517, Old York Road
London SW18 1TF
0181 874 8500

Academy of Food and Wine Service
Burgoine House,
Burgoine Quay
8, Lower Teddington Road
Kingston upon Thames KT1 4ER
0181 977 4419

British Hospitality Association
Queens House
55–56, Lincolns Inn Fields
London WC2A 3BH
0171 404 7744

Hotel and Catering, International
Management Association
191, Trinity Road
London SW17 7HN
0181 672 4251

Restaurateurs' Association of Great
Britain
28, Kingsway
London WC2B 6JR
0171 831 8727

Wine and Spirit Education Trust
Five Kings House
1, Queens Street Place
London EC4R 1XX
0171 236 3551

Other information sources

City and Guilds of London Institute
1, Guiltspur Street
London EC1A 9DD
0171 294 2468

Hospitality Help Line
0891 44 33 22 (premium rate service)

Hospitality Training Foundation
International House,
High Street
Ealing
London W5 5DB
0181 579 2400

Her Majesty's Stationery Office (HMSO)
Belfast 01232 238451
Birmingham 0121 236 9696
Bristol 0117 926 4306
Edinburgh 0131 228 4181
London 0171 873 0011
Manchester 0161 833 0634

The World Wide Web
Internet service offering an incredibly vast
amount of freely available information on
hospitality companies and all aspects of
food and beverages.